HONEY UNLEASHED

FAMILY OF RESCUE DOGS
BOOK 9

BRIAN L. PORTER

Honey Unleashed

DEDICATION

Honey Unleashed is dedicated to the memory of all the dogs, who at the beginning of this series, were a part of our wonderful pack of rescues, and who have sadly crossed the Rainbow Bridge over the years it has taken me to write this collection of dog tales. So, it is with much love that this dedication is an affectionate remembrance of Sasha, Dexter, Penny, Dylan, Sheba, and Muttley, who passed away just as I was about to write the final chapter of this book, all of whose stories have featured in the series. The sadness we have felt at the loss of our beautiful dogs who were all much loved members of our family lives with us every day and we can truly say that they have all left their indelible pawprints on our hearts.

Loving memories of Dexter, Sasha, Dylan, Penny, and Sheba

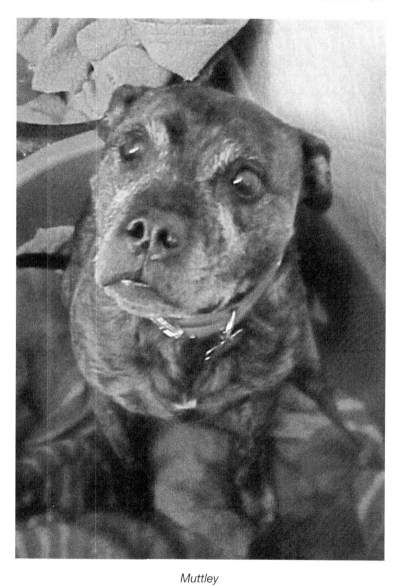

Muttley

INTRODUCTION

Welcome to *Honey Unleashed,* the ninth book in my Family of Rescue Dogs series. Honey is the youngest member of our family, but her story is one of such fun and laughter that I hope you'll enjoy reading it as much as I've enjoyed writing it. In a way, I'm quite sad to be writing this book, as it looks like being the final episode in the series that has chronicled the lives and adventures of the dogs that have been such an important part in the lives of our own human family, and yet, there's a little surprise for you at the end of the book which could eventually lead to yet another book. As you'll soon be reading, Honey's arrival in our home was completely unplanned and was a total surprise to Juliet and me. How, you might ask, can a dog's arrival in our home have been such a surprise? All I can suggest is that you read and hopefully enjoy the story of this little girl who so quickly wormed her way into our hearts.

Honey's story coincides with some of the most turbulent and sad times for our family of rescue dogs, as she has grown up and lived through the tragic losses of six of the dogs who were present when she joined the family, all due to old age and infir-

mity. How Honey has coped with the ever-changing composi-
tion of our canine family is a perfect example of the way this
wonderfully happy little dog has adapted and continued to
enjoy her life with us.

Honey

1

A CHRISTMAS SURPRISE

THE YEAR WAS 2017, and as the end of November approached and the weather grew colder with the onset of winter, Juliet and I were planning our first Christmas without either of the girls being at home with us. Rebecca was by now studying at Leeds Beckett University and was living in a shared house in that city with two other students, and Victoria was by now living with her long-time boyfriend, and working for an insurance company so the house was now ours to enjoy as we saw fit, together with our canine family of course.

Victoria had only moved out a couple of months ago and was living with her boyfriend a few miles from home. During her last few months at home, she'd almost constantly asked Juliet and me if we could get another dog. Victoria has always been 'dog mad' so this was just typical of her. As we felt we'd got enough dogs to keep us busy for years to come we'd repeatedly told her, "No Victoria. We really don't need any more dogs in the house at the moment."

On the day in question, Juliet and I had just fed the dogs when Victoria walked into the house through the front door.

"Oh, hello, what are you doing here?" Juliet asked her.

"Mum, I need you to come outside for a minute," Victoria replied.

"Why, what's wrong?" Juliet asked, thinking that something bad must have happened.

"Nothing's wrong, but I really need you to come outside with me, Mum."

Juliet dutifully followed Victoria out through the front door while I stayed with the dogs, and a few minutes later, she walked back into the house carrying a tiny, furry bundle in her arms, followed by Victoria carrying a dog bed and a bag containing various unknown items.

"What's this then?" I asked.

"Apparently this is our Christmas present from Victoria," Juliet replied.

"Oh, Victoria, what have we said about not wanting any more dogs?"

Victoria just looked at me with a huge grin on her face. I looked at the little puppy nestled in Juliet's arms and there was no doubting that it was a very cute little dog. Despite feeling slightly angry at Victoria for ignoring us with regards to adding to our doggie family, it was impossible to look at that happy little face and not instantly fall in love with her. Things Victoria had previously told her Mum now began to make sense. A few weeks previously, she'd told her Mum that a friend's dog had given birth to a litter of puppies and she, (Victoria) was helping her to look after them till they were old enough to go to new homes. She'd even shown Juliet some photos of the puppies and asked her which one she liked the best. Juliet, unsuspectingly, pointed out one of the puppies, though it wasn't the one that she now held in her arms.

While Victoria went in the lounge as her Mum instructed her and placed the dog bed and blanket with numerous toys in it on the carpet, Juliet brought the puppy closer to me so I could say hello to our very special, surprise Christmas present. Victoria called from the lounge, saying "Her name is Honey by the way." Sneaky Victoria had even named her for us so there was no going back on that score.

Juliet and I spent a few minutes examining little Honey. She was very tiny and cuddly, a bright honey-coloured coat showing just why Victoria had come up with the name. Honey seemed to have lots of loose skin and at first, we could have been forgiven for thinking she was partly Shar Pei, there were so many folds.

"What breed is she supposed to be?" Juliet asked Victoria who by now had joined us in the hallway.

"She's supposed to be half Staffy," came the reply.

"And what about the other half?" I asked.

"Erm, they're not sure," she replied.

"Oh, great. So, she could be half Husky for all we know," I grinned.

"What about her injections, insurance and so on?" Juliet asked her.

"Oh, I'll pay for those and for the insurance," Victoria promised. "You can get that Vac for Life deal, can't you?"

Honey has just celebrated her 4th birthday and I'm still waiting for Victoria to pay the promised fees for injections and insurance, not that I would have taken it from her anyway...lol.

Our vet has a scheme whereby you can make a one-off payment of £99, and it will cover all the dog's injections and annual boosters for the duration of its life.

"Yes, I'll call the vet in the morning and get her booked in. Exactly how old is she?"

"She's eight weeks old."

"Okay, let's have a good look at her," I said, and Juliet put the puppy down on the floor. Straight away, our Cassie came out of the lounge to see what was going on. Wow, did she have a shock when she saw the puppy. She walked up to Honey, followed by Penny, sniffed her, then turned around and ran back into the lounge and hid under the coffee table. Penny, who got on well with every other dog we'd ever owned, wagged her tail, had a quick sniff, and went back to the lounge and went back to her bed. Cassie and Penny, being elderly, were allowed to spend the daytime in the lounge, to give them some peace from the boisterous activities of the rest of the pack.

"Oh dear, poor Cassie's not impressed," I smiled as I spoke.

"I'm sure she'll soon get used to her," Juliet responded.

Thinking practically, I next asked, "And where is she going to sleep at night?"

"We'll have to use the crate," Juliet replied, referring to the crate we'd bought when Sasha was a puppy and we needed somewhere to keep her inactive while she recuperated from her broken leg, (twice). We'd kept the crate since we'd last used it (When Muffin, Digby, and Petal were puppies) and it was currently residing in the shed in the back garden. After retrieving it and bringing it indoors, Juliet spent some time cleaning it and making sure it was suitable for the puppy to use as sleeping accommodation. As luck would have it, the bed that Victoria had bought for Honey was a perfect fit for the crate, so that was one problem quickly and easily solved.

Honey's first photo

The next big test was now upon us. The rest of our dogs had seen the puppy in the hall as they had a clear view through the baby gate that separated the kitchen from the hall. They were already showing signs of interest in the little puppy, and we were obviously a little anxious as to how they'd react when they met Honey, face to face. We decided the best place to allow them to meet Honey was the kitchen, where there was lots of space. Would we separate some of the dogs and introduce Honey gradually, or would we let them all meet her together?

Knowing that Sheba and Muttley could be rather boisterous, we decided to keep them apart from the others while we introduced Honey to them, and we put those two out in the garden until the first introductions were made. Juliet picked little Honey up and carried her into the kitchen and placed her on the floor. Instantly her little tail began wagging with excitement as the other dogs gathered around her, all showing great interest in the puppy in their midst. They all seemed to welcome Honey without any problem, so we decided to allow Sheba and Muttley to come and say hello. Much to our surprise, the two powerful Staffies appeared to recognise that Honey was just a baby, and they said their hellos quite gently, with noses touching and tails wagging.

Honey was so excited to meet all her new doggie friends and then, we were witness to a wonderful moment. Sasha, who some years earlier had sort of 'adopted' Muffin, Digby, and Petal when they arrived as puppies in our house and acted as a 'surrogate' mother to the pups, now decided to do the same thing with Honey. Before we knew it, she was in one of the beds in the kitchen, with little Honey snuggled up to her.

Sasha with baby Honey

As you can see from the photograph Sasha looked so happy to have a 'new' puppy to take care of. She really did have a wonderful maternal instinct and in the coming weeks she did exactly the same with Honey as she'd previously done with Muffin, Digby, and Petal. Honey definitely loved her 'new' Mummy and Sasha spent so much time with her, 'teaching' her how to behave in the home, so much so that, as with the previous puppies, Honey needed virtually no house training from us. When Sasha went outside, Honey would happily trot along behind her, and Juliet and I would watch them inter-acting together in the garden. If Sasha did a pee, Honey would copy her, and she soon learned that if she needed to 'go to the toilet' she would have to go outside to 'do it'. It was quite amazing really. Sasha had done all this before of course and it did lead us to wonder just how Sasha managed to communicate all the various required information to her new baby.

Not only that, but Sasha would spend hours happily playing with Honey, and Honey of course loved every minute, as Sasha would allow the puppy to jump all over her, rag her ears and even chew Sasha's legs as though they were actual dog toys. Juliet and I couldn't help laughing as we watched the way they played together and very soon the other dogs would join in the games which provided us with so much laughter and entertainment. Sasha and Sheba had always enjoyed playing together and would often engage in games of roly-poly together, which was always so funny as Sheba was quite ungainly when she rolled onto her back, but this game now became even more amusing, as little Honey decided it looked like fun and suddenly leaped on top of the two adult dogs and joined in the game. It was hilarious.

The next thing that brought smiles to our faces was when, one afternoon, we saw Honey sitting up in one of the dog beds which was positioned on the floor not far from our fish tank. She had her front paws resting on the ledge of the bed, and was completely entranced, watching the fish swimming around. Juliet and I also noticed that as she watched them, her tail was wagging with happiness. If that had been a 'one-off' occurrence it would have been funny enough, but from that time, Honey would frequently return to that bed and happily spend ages just enjoying watching the fish. We were so amused by this that we dubbed it 'Honey TV'. Watching the fish zooming around in their tank had quickly become Honey's favourite 'show'.

2

HONEY'S PRIZE

THE DAY ARRIVED for Honey to pay her visit to the vet for her first injections. Having made an early morning appointment, I arrived at the surgery just after 8.30 am. The staff in reception were absolutely delighted to meet the latest addition to our 'pack'. They were all enamoured with the excited little puppy that I carried in to meet them all. They of course knew all our dogs and apart from the receptionist who'd taken my original call to book the appointment, they were totally surprised to meet this latest addition to our canine family.

Of course, puppies do have a habit of attracting attention and lots of fuss, and Honey was no exception. Her little tail was wagging ten to the dozen and she was passed from one receptionist to another, quickly joined by a couple of the practice nurses who happened to walk into the reception area as they were smothering Honey with hugs, strokes, and kisses. Honey was loving all the attention and her little face was a picture as she lapped up all the attention.

I just about managed to calm her down by the time the vet called us in to the consulting room.

"What a little beauty," she enthused on meeting Honey for the first time. Do you know her background?"

"As far as we know, she's part staffy, but we don't know what else is in there," I laughed as I spoke.

"With all this loose skin you could be forgiven for thinking there's some Shar Pei in her ancestry," the vet said, "but it's hard to say for sure at this age. You'll have to wait and see how she develops."

"We're not really bothered too much," I replied. "She's just a beautiful little puppy and we're happy to have her."

We were only in there for a few minutes, as the vet gave Honey her first injections and a quick all-over examination to ensure she was perfectly healthy. Before leaving the surgery, I stopped at reception again, made an appointment for her to return for her second injections in two weeks' time, and of course, a chance for the staff to make even more fuss of our new 'baby'. I paid the fee for Honey to have the 'vac for life' so we'd never have to pay for her annual boosters for the rest of her life, and we set off for home, having made an appointment for her to have her second round of injections, where Sasha and the rest of the dogs gave Honey a big welcome home. Already, she was extremely popular with the rest of the dogs and Honey just couldn't wait to get out into the garden and play with her doggie friends, Sasha in particular, who was soon romping around with 'her' puppy.

While I'd been at the vet, Victoria had phoned her Mum and had arranged to come and spend the night at home with us so she could spend some time with Honey. Sure enough, she duly arrived after finishing work for the day and Honey was clearly pleased to see her and Victoria made such a fuss of her, with Honey again relishing all the attention she was receiving. This was one popular puppy!

Later that evening Victoria went upstairs for a shower and

when she came back downstairs little Honey did her best to try and jump up and sit on Victoria's lap for a cuddle, but she was still too small to manage the leap. Her little legs were just too short, but she did her best, and eventually Victoria had to pick her up and she was soon cuddled up on Victoria's lap. Mission accomplished!

Doing her best to jump on Victoria's lap

During the next two weeks, little Honey seemed to grow quite fast. One thing we soon realised was that she was getting longer, but not much taller. In fact, she soon had Juliet and I convinced that she must have a touch of dachshund in her genetic make-up. Her legs remained short and stocky, and her body gradually began to fill out, and the folds of loose skin were gradually beginning to disappear. Juliet joked that "Her body's starting to fill her skin at last."

When we returned to the vet for Honey's second vaccinations, even the staff who'd seen her on her first visit, commented on her progress.

"Wow, Mr Porter, she's grown quite a lot already, hasn't she?" one of the receptionists observed, and the vet confirmed that comment when we went into the consulting room. She even added, "She's getting longer, isn't she?" reinforcing what Juliet and I had already noticed.

I mentioned our dachshund theory and the vet replied, "I think we might never know exactly what Honey's ancestry is, but as long as she's a happy and healthy dog that's all that matters," which of course, I agreed with.

It was during those first few weeks that I saw a Facebook post, inviting dog owners to submit photos of their dogs to a photographer, with the prize being a beautiful canvas print of the winning dog. Just for fun, I entered Honey's first puppy photo and also one of my favourite photos of Sasha. I was surprised and delighted a couple of weeks later, when I received an email informing me that the photographer liked the photos of Honey and Sasha so much that he wanted to name them as joint winners of the competition and asked for my home address so he could have canvases made of both photos to send to me. Both of those photos still have pride of place on the wall in our hallway, just inside the house so they are the first thing people see when they walk through our front door.

Honey

Honey and Sasha's prizewinning canvases

Juliet and I were obviously extremely proud of both dogs, and it seemed appropriate that both Honey and her 'surrogate' Mother, Sasha had jointly earned the prize. Honey continued to develop and now that she was fully vaccinated, we were able to take our new puppy out into the big wide world. Honey was about to make lots of new friends.

Cute puppy

3

THE DRAUGHT EXCLUDER TERRIER

WE AGREED THAT, as my health meant I was by now forced to walk with the aid of a walking stick, that Juliet would be responsible for taking Honey for the majority of her walks, so she could be let off the lead, once fully trained, and she'd be able to run and play with the other dogs on the playing field, both our own dogs, and any new friends she'd make on those walks. I would take her for occasional short lead walks with Cassie or Sasha early in the morning just to make sure she was used to walking with different members of the pack.

Within days of Juliet taking her on the local playing field, Honey was already gathering a whole load of new doggie friends and our personal friends quickly fell in love with the little puppy. Thanks to Sasha's influence, Honey proved extremely easy to train. She soon learned the basics, such as sit, stay, come here etc and in record time, Juliet felt confident enough to let her run free and make friends with everyone. Honey just loved the freedom that came with being allowed to run free, her little legs carrying her at an amazing pace as she scampered along with all her new friends. People were amazed at how fast the little puppy could run and she soon developed a wonderful character as a loving and playful little pup.

Our pretty puppy, a perfect 'sit' at 10 weeks old

Of course, an often-repeated question at that time from people meeting her for the first time was, "What breed is she?"

Neither Juliet nor I could provide a definitive answer to the question but could only explain what we knew of her ancestry, which wasn't much to be honest. As the weeks went by, and Honey continued to grow, we couldn't help arriving at the conclusion that although she was growing longer, but her legs stayed the same short length and her body was filling out, showing her to be rather solid and muscular, obviously her staffy ancestry was partially responsible for that side of her development. To us, she was still our little, tiny puppy but even then, we wondered just how large she'd eventually become. One day, when a friend asked me the usual question about her breed I quickly replied, "She's a draught excluder terrier," which had become a private joke between Juliet and me, referring to her long body, and short legs, making her the ideal size to help eliminate draughts if she lay across the bottom of a door. That name quickly seemed to stick with her and very soon some of our friends, seeing Juliet and Honey approaching would laughingly shout, "Look out, here comes the draught excluder terrier."

The draught excluder

Honey was such a happy puppy. Playing with Sasha was her favourite pastime, and it gave Juliet and me immense pleasure to watch her romping, rolling, and playing 'chase' and doing zoomies together with Sasha in the garden. The only problem was that the two of them also decided to do 'zoomies' indoors as well, which created quite a bit of havoc in the kitchen where the wood-laminate flooring made them slip and slide and bump into the other dogs, our legs, and items of furniture. Incredibly, both Sasha and Honey never seemed to hurt themselves when they banged into the legs of the dining table, or worse still, flew headlong into the kitchen cabinets or even solid walls!

Now that she was a few weeks older, she decided she was going to insert herself into the lives and the playtimes of Muffin, Digby, and Petal. The three siblings who we'd adopted together from one litter were by now 6 years old and from being tiny puppies themselves, had spent their lives doing virtually everything together, so much so that we thought of them as 'one dog with twelve legs', they were so inseparable. Honey had given herself a monumental task, in attempting to become a part of their 'inner circle.' They'd always allowed her to join in some of their games and in time, Juliet began taking Honey for walks with one or two of them to allow her to fully integrate with them.

As soon as Juliet started taking Honey for walks with 'the puppies' the name we still refer to them as at ten years old, it became obvious that Honey was a 'hit' with everyone she met. Juliet's friends, who she'd meet up with on her afternoon dog walk all fell in love with her in no time at all. Juliet would come home from those afternoon walks with a big smile on her face, and she enjoyed regaling me with the tales of Honey's adventures with all her new doggie pals. Aside from the time they'd spend on the playing field with all the other local dogs and their owners, Juliet would occasionally give the field a miss and would instead take Honey and Digby, or Muffin to the local woods where she'd let them have a really good time, running free. Honey especially loved setting her sights on a squirrel or maybe a rabbit, which she'd set off in chase of, (never catching one of course). Juliet wouldn't have been very happy if she'd succeeded in those chases.

On returning home, it was clear to me that the dogs, Honey in particular had enjoyed themselves immensely. Honey's tail would be wagging furiously, even as she took a big drink from the water bowl. It seemed like nothing could interfere with Honey's tail wagging celebration of a great playtime or walk. Of course, after the walk and a big drink, it was always time for a short rest before feeding time would be upon us and Honey soon got used to flopping down on the cool wooden floor with one or two of the other dogs, who were readily accepting her as 'one of the gang,' as young as she was.

Puppy Honey with Muffin and Petal

Like all puppies, Honey was growing fast, but we were still amazed that she continued to grow longer, (including her tail), but her height stayed pretty much the same. Her body did show signs of growing heavier, with a stocky, muscular build, it just wasn't matched with equal growth of her little legs, which more than anything, continued to give her a particularly dachshund-like appearance. Bearing in mind her age, Juliet and I still thought that she had plenty of time to develop and 'expand' into a larger dog. Time would prove us wrong of course.

It goes without saying that Honey was a typical puppy, happy, excitable, inquisitive, and playful. Sometimes, just watching her playing with the other dogs could make you tired. She was so fast, doing zoomies round the garden, just for the sheer joy of it, her tail always held up proudly, and a look of complete happiness on her little face.

Zoom!

Of course, playtime for puppies usually involves toys, and Honey was no exception. The only problem we had was trying to find her some toys that could withstand more than about ten minutes before being completely destroyed by 'the Honey Monster' as she had such strong teeth and jaws, even at such a

young age that even the so-called 'tough' toys for dogs didn't
stand a chance against her. The only toy that seemed to last her
more than a week was a pretty tough hard rubber bone that she
had great fun with, while it lasted. Fellow dog owners will, I'm
sure, have seen the so-called 'super-tough', 'unbreakable' toys
for dogs that have appeared on the market in recent years. This
one lasted Honey for around three or four weeks before being
consigned to the home for destroyed dog toys. The makers of
those 'unbreakable' toys had obviously never met our Honey!

Honey with her 'unbreakable' bone

* * *

ONE DAY, we discovered a new game for Honey, completely by accident. Due to my personal disabilities, I was forced to use a very long shoe horn to help me in putting on my shoes or trainers. This particular morning, Juliet and I couldn't stop laughing when little Honey walked into the kitchen, head held high, carrying my stainless-steel shoehorn in her mouth, as if it was a giant stick. She looked so proud of herself, as she walked up to me and dropped the shoehorn at my feet, looking up at me as if to say, "Aren't I clever?" Over the next few days, Honey repeatedly went to the shoe rack where the shoehorn was kept handily nearby and picked up or dragged the 18-inch-long shoe horn and seemed to have great fun trying to play with it. Because of the length of it, she couldn't carry it too far without it bumping into the furniture and in doing so it would be knocked out of her mouth and she began to get frustrated with her inability to hang on to it for long. I decided to try and find her something more suited to her size, so a quick visit to eBay provided what I thought would be the perfect solution to the problem. I found, and bought a pair of smaller, 6-inch-long shoe horns that I thought would be the ideal, really unbreakable toys for her.

Success! Honey loved her new toys, and as she celebrates her 5th birthday in October, it's incredible that after all this time, both shoe horns are still in one piece and remain Honey's favourite toys to this day!

The only competition she has with her shoe horns is that Muffin has also discovered they make good toys too and she'll quite often pick up one of Honey's toys and run off with it, usually taking it to a bed and lying there happily chewing on it until Honey realises she's got it and then does her best to get it back from her. Honey is never aggressive though and tries to 'threaten' Muffin by standing in front of her, with her tail wagging slowly, and sometimes making a strange noise, which could never be called a growl, in her efforts to get the shoehorn away from Muffin. Eventually, I think Muffin just gets bored with it and she'll usually just get up and leave the bed with the shoehorn in it as she wanders off to find something else with which to amuse herself.

Honey with her shoe horn 'toy'

4

HONEY'S HOME ENTERTAINMENT

ANYONE WHO HAS EVER WELCOMED a puppy into their home will know what fun it can be watching and enjoying the development of their little dog as it gradually assumes its own personality and identity and engages with the family and in our case, a house full of other dogs. Having said that, even a happy and lively puppy sometimes needs their own moments of peace and quiet, and Honey was no exception.

One day, I walked into the dining room, where we have a fish tank in the corner of the room. I had to smile when I saw Honey sitting up in the nearest dog bed to the fish tank, quite obviously watching the fish swimming around, with great interest. She seemed to be mesmerised by the comings and goings of our finny friends and before we knew it, watching the fish became a regular pastime for the little puppy, so much so that we dubbed her time watching the fish as her watching 'Honey TV'. She literally spent ages just sitting, enthralled by the peaceful sight of the fish as they gently navigated their way around the tank, in and around the plants and ornaments.

Quite often, she'd sit there for so long that we would see her eyes gradually beginning to close and she'd suddenly go from sitting to lying down, eventually falling asleep after being 'hypnotised' to sleep by the graceful meanderings of our five fishy pets.

Soon after she'd discovered 'Honey TV' we had to laugh a few days later when we saw Honey's latest source of entertainment...the washing machine! One morning, Juliet said to me, "Where's Honey?" I replied, "I don't know", and went to look for our inquisitive puppy, wondering what mischief she might be up to. Walking into the utility room, I was amused at what I saw, and quietly called Juliet to come and see. There was little Honey, avidly watching the washing machine in action, her eyes following the drum as it rotated with the clothes moving around inside it. Having discovered the incredibly interesting entertainment provided by the washing machine, it quickly became another of little Honey's favourite pastimes. Whenever Juliet put the washing machine on, we only had to wait a few minutes for Honey to realise it was operating, and there she'd be, watching the machine in action.

Watching the washing!

It was so funny to see her, as she seemed to be concentrating so hard as she watched the washing machine operating, her head would move from side to side as if she was following the movement of the rotating drum, and every so often her tail would give a couple of wags, as if she was getting excited at whatever she was seeing.

Honey was proving to us that she was a very intelligent little dog, who was extremely interested in everything that was going on in the world around her. Now that she'd grown a little, she soon found out that she had the ability to jump up on the sofa when we allowed all the dogs into the lounge with us in the evening. She loved cuddling up beside Juliet, or with the other dogs who would share the sofa with Juliet and each other. It was now that Honey made a new and exciting discovery...television!

When she realised that Juliet was sometimes sitting engrossed in watching something that wasn't her, she must have decided to take a look at whatever was taking her Mum's attention away from herself. One evening, as Juliet was watching one of her favourite programmes on the TV, I looked across from my armchair, where Sasha was comfortably snuggled up on my lap, to see that Honey had found herself a new position and had propped herself up beside Juliet to watch the TV. She looked so relaxed as though she was really enjoying whatever she was seeing on the screen. Juliet and I couldn't help laughing at her, once again looking so intelligent.

"This dog is too intelligent by far," Juliet commented one day, with a big smile on her face as Honey sat propped up against the back of the sofa watching one of Juliet's favourite programmes with her. Honestly, the look on Honey's face, as she watched an episode of *Come Dine With Me* was just so intense. It was as if she understood every word that was being spoken on the TV.

"Maybe she likes watching all that food being prepared and served up," I quipped, at which point Honey turned her head briefly in my direction before returning her gaze to the TV, as if she was saying, "Can you be quiet please? I'm trying to watch this programme." I agreed with Juliet regarding Honey's intelligence. She definitely seems to know what we're talking about, therefore she probably understands the words coming from the big screen in the corner of the room.

Watching the telly!

Maybe we had a doggie genius on our hands! She certainly had a habit of turning up in the kitchen, not just if we were cooking, but just hearing us talking about food seemed to do the trick, as we'd hear this little figure padding across the wooden floor, and sitting behind us as if she was asking, "Anything for me?" The look on her face when she did this was just so precious.

"And just what are you doing here, young lady?" Juliet would ask, and in return, Honey would do a perfect sit and look up at her with her tail furiously wagging as if we were supposed to understand perfectly well why she'd suddenly appeared behind us.

Without a doubt, Honey was an extremely intelligent puppy who was not just capable of finding ways to entertain herself, but who also seemed to know how to engage with us in finding new ways to keep her happy.

* * *

This is a good time to tell you about one of Honey's cutest traits. Each morning, Juliet and I wake up at around 5.30 am and Juliet is the first to make her way downstairs, where she puts the kettle on to make tea for her and coffee for me. Without fail, the first to greet her is little Honey, who always runs to her and Juliet bends down to make a fuss of her. Once she stands up again, Honey then sits directly in front of her and makes little squeaky noises and at the same time she does what we call 'paddy paws' as she does a kind of little dance with her front paws bouncing up and down while she carries on her vocal greeting to Juliet. I usually follow a few minutes later and Honey gives me exactly the same greeting. I wish there was a way I could illustrate this for you, the reader, as it's something we've never experienced with any of our other dogs. It's incredibly cute and she's now carried out this little morning ritual of hers for years and I doubt she'll ever stop it. I think it's a sign of the love and trust that Honey feels for us both.

1ˢᵗ birthday

Before I forget, I must mention Honey's bark. Bear in mind her size, and you'll understand how, the first time we heard her bark, when we were both indoors and she was in the garden, we had no idea who was responsible for the incredibly deep, loud barking coming from the garden. When we went outside, we were astounded to find that the barking was coming from Honey! Seriously, our little pup had the bark of a rottweiler or some other large breed of dog. With the passage of time, Honey's bark has definitely not grown any quieter and Juliet often returns from one of her long afternoon walks with Honey with tales to tell me of how people have been utterly surprised and amazed, having heard barking from afar, only to eventually come into view and realise that what they were hearing has been this little dog who must have the lungs of a lion.

Honey and her bone

5

A SENSE OF LOSS

SOMETIMES, it was easy to forget just how young little Honey was. She was definitely of above average intelligence for a young dog but that did nothing to take away her exuberance and sheer joy of everyday life, especially when she was enjoying herself in the company of Sasha, who continued to provide Honey with her special love in her self-appointed role as Honey's surrogate mum. Seeing them together, reminded us how small Honey was, and how much growing up she still had to do.

Honey with 'Mummy' Sasha

Honey soon made it quite obvious that she was destined to be a 'mummy's girl' in much the same way that Digby was a definite 'mummy's boy'. She'd follow Juliet around the house and hated to be parted from her for any length of time. If she felt she wasn't receiving the attention she felt she deserved, Honey would come up behind Juliet and with one paw, she'd scrape her paw down the back of Juliet's leg. Due to the fact her claws were quite sharp, it wasn't unusual for me to hear Juliet to cry out, "Honey, no, that hurts." Juliet would then turn around and look down at the offending puppy who'd be sitting on the floor behind her, wagging her tail with happiness because she'd succeeded in getting her Mum's attention. Of course, Juliet couldn't be angry with her little girl, and would make a fuss of her before carrying on with whatever she was doing before being interrupted by 'the paw'.

Honey has just passed her fifth birthday and she still uses the same attention-seeking ploy. She's now developed an advanced method of gaining attention if Juliet happens to be out shopping or walking any of the other dogs. She now turns her attention to me instead. The backs of my legs have thus become similar victims to Juliet's, and I'm now quite used to receiving 'the paw' treatment if she's feeling 'neglected'.

Sadly, I now have to go back to the time when Honey was approaching her third birthday. Having spent so much time with Sasha, playing, learning from her, and cuddling up when she needed a 'loving touch', Honey was as close to Sasha as it was possible to be. Those of you who may have read Sasha's story, or who have followed my Family of Rescue Dogs series on Facebook, will know that Sasha had suffered from canine epilepsy, from the age of two and a half years. Poor Sasha literally suffered from hundreds of epileptic seizures during her life, yet she always recovered from each seizure and would carry on as though nothing had happened. My personal relationship with Sasha was unlike that between me and any other dog I've ever owned. We had an incredible bond, which was probably so strong due to the two occasions in her first year when she broke the same leg, twice. Following the operations to rebuild her shattered elbow joint, she had to spend up to three months recuperating in a crate in the kitchen, only being allowed out to, feeling lonely, I spent most of that time sitting in a garden chair at the side of her crate, talking to her, playing gently with her through the bars of the crate, giving her little treats and so on. The other dogs would of course come round and try to interact with her through the bars, but it wasn't the same as being able to play properly with the little puppy. As time went by, Sasha and I grew incredibly close to the extent that when she was fully recovered, she would only go for walks with me.

Poor Juliet was kind of excluded and Sasha became 'my' dog. I should mention that I suffer from angina, and in time, Sasha developed the ability to predict when I was about to have an angina attack. She had a way to warn me when an attack was imminent and would keep nudging my leg until I went into the lounge and put my feet up on the sofa. Once I was there, she'd jump up with me and drape herself over my legs, not moving at all until the attack came and passed. Once she was sure I was okay, she'd jump down from the sofa and proudly sit looking up me with her tail wagging as if to say, *"Okay Dad, you can come and play again now."* She really was quite an incredible dog.

A cuddle from Sasha

This wonderful dog tragically left our lives in July 2000. It was a lovely, warm summer's day and Sasha, together with our other dogs was lying on the cushions we placed in the garden for the dogs, enjoying soaking up the sun. I'd checked on them all just before Juliet and I sat down to eat our lunch. When I went outside again after eating, I found Sasha still lying in the same position, and when I walked up to her and went to stroke her, I found her to be unresponsive to my touch, something totally unheard of. We quickly loaded her into the car, first calling ahead to the vet to tell them to expect us.

It transpired that my beautiful, loving Sasha had suffered a massive stroke while 'sunbathing' in the garden, and I was with her as the vet gave her the injection that brought her life to an end. The only consolation I could gain from her end, was that at least she didn't suffer, and she passed away in one of her favourite places, happy and relaxed in the summer sunshine.

In the days that followed Sasha's death, I was personally consumed by intense grief. Sasha and I had been virtually inseparable for nearly ten years, and I freely admit that I cried tears of grief almost non-stop for a week, as I found it so difficult to cope without my very special girl by my side. As for the dogs, they soon proved that they too have feelings as they displayed their own grief in their own way.

Both Sheba and Honey immediately began to display their feelings when it became obvious to them that Sasha hadn't returned home with me.

Sheba & Sasha, Best friends forever

Even though Sheba was older than Sasha by some years, I think the fact that Sheba had undergone such a terrible start in life, being used as a bait dog by dog fighters, left her with feelings of insecurity and when we brought Sasha into the family, and Sasha grew to adulthood, the two dogs rapidly became best friends, with Sheba seeming to depend on Sasha as her protector. Sasha's natural maternal qualities obviously extended to taking care of an abused and needy dog like Sheba. Sheba would follow Sasha around, enjoyed playing with her and wherever Sasha was in the house or garden, we could be certain that Sheba wouldn't be far away from her.

Sasha had become Sheba's 'rock' who she depended upon as though Sasha would always be there to help Sheba stay safe and happy. I'd take the pair of them for walks together and it was truly one of the highlights of my day to see them walking side by side, with Sheba every so often casting a sideways glance at Sasha as if to make sure she was still there beside her.

Our afternoon walk would usually coincide with the children coming out of school. The two dogs gradually developed a wonderful rapport with the children and it was great to see the children, mostly aged between 8 and 10 years old, running to see their two doggie friends. Sasha and Sheba's tails would wag furiously with excitement when they saw the children running to see them. The dogs definitely helped some parents to realise that Staffies didn't deserve the reputation some people attached to them, of being nasty, vicious dogs. No dogs could have been as gentle with children, or indeed with the elderly, as Sasha and Sheba.

Sasha & Sheba's last photo together

For Honey, the loss of Sasha really affected her from the moment I returned from the vet without her by my side. Poor little Honey immediately began looking for her 'Mummy' and couldn't understand where Sasha was. As much as we were all grieving over the loss of our beautiful Sasha, Honey literally spent the first few days after Sasha's death searching for her. We could tell by the way she'd walk around the house and the garden, obviously looking for something, or someone. Every time someone came into the house, and she heard the door opening or closing, she'd run to see who it was, and both Juliet and I soon worked out in our own minds that Honey was looking for Sasha. Poor Honey. Sasha had been her surrogate Mother, her chief playmate and 'teacher' of all manner of 'doggie' behaviours from the day Honey had entered our home and our lives, and now she was gone. I estimate that Honey went through about a month of severely missing Sasha, and it really was quite distressing for us to see how much both Sheba and Honey were affected by Sasha's loss. Don't let anyone ever tell us that dogs don't have feelings!

All the other dogs seemed to know that Sasha wasn't coming home again and Muttley and Muffin, Digby and Petal, Dylan, Penny, and Cassie who had all felt Sasha's immense presence in our home and in their lives appeared to feel the massive sense of loss that we all experienced during that time. Juliet and I always kind of felt that Sasha was indestructible, such was her strength of character and her bravery in coping with the epilepsy, her broken legs and everything else that our wonderfully resilient little girl went through during her time with us.

This was our second loss in just over a year, as we'd previously lost our beautiful Labrador/Staffy, Dexter during the previous year, after he'd fought a long battle against heart and lung disease. So many people had followed his story on Facebook that I received multiple requests to write his story next. I did, and *Remembering Dexter* became a bestseller on the day it was released.

Dexter had earned himself the nickname of our 'bird-dog' due to the incredible affinity he had with the wild birds that visited our garden, even allowing sparrows to perch on his back as he lay in the sun, under the bird table. After his death, I created 'Dexter's Memorial Garden' in his memory, a special place where the birds could come and feed, find shelter, and feel safe.

Dexter with his favourite toy

6

THE FOURTH MUSKETEER, AND AN UNEXPECTED OPERATION

WITH DEXTER AND Sasha gone from our lives it took a while, but gradually life returned to normality, and gradually, our little pack of rescues began to take on a new dynamic. Without Sasha, little Honey had to find new ways to entertain herself. She'd always enjoyed joining in playtimes with any and all of our other dogs, particularly with Muffin, Digby, and Petal, who we still referred to as the three puppies, as we continue to refer to them even today, despite them having just this week passed their eleventh birthday. From the time they'd entered our family those three pups had always spent most of their time together, so much so that we began to talk about them being like 'one dog with twelve legs.' They were simply inseparable and went through life doing virtually everything together, whether it be walking, playing, sleeping or, well, just about everything.

Honey, who enjoyed interacting with them whenever she could, now decided she kind of liked spending her time with them and began inserting herself into their games and dog play at every opportunity. The three pups certainly displayed no objection to Honey becoming part of their regular play routines and before we knew it, Honey's tail was once again in 'full speed wag mode' once more.

Digby, Honey, and Muffin

Muffin, Digby, and Petal, being of a completely friendly nature, lost no time in accepting Honey as part of their self-styled 'play group' and Honey definitely enjoyed inserting herself into their company. We'd always seen the three pups as being a kind of 'private' club, sort of like the three musketeers, an 'all for one and one for all' little group. Now, as Honey became more and more a regular part of their group, our 'three musketeers' had become four, so it was only natural that we decided to describe Honey as the fourth musketeer, a D'Artagnan to the puppies Athos, Porthos and Aramis. Sometimes I'm sure the pups must have wondered what had hit them, as 'Honey the Hurricane' swept into their lives like a veritable tsunami of youthful energy!

Put quite simply, Muffin, Digby and Petal absolutely loved it when Honey decided to join in their playtimes and doggy games. They immediately embraced the addition to their fun times and our 'fourth musketeer' certainly took advantage of the great fun she now enjoyed with the older dogs. To be fair, Honey not only enjoyed playing with Muffin and Co, but she spread her sociability around, as she would often engage with Sheba and occasionally with Muttley too, doing her best to include them in her playful activities. To be fair, it has to be said that both Sheba and Muttley were considerably older than the rest of our dogs, with Sheba in particular already suffering from quite serious arthritis which tended to limit the amount of time and energy she had to play with Honey, but to her credit, Sheba always did the best she could when Honey decided it was playtime.

It was around this time when we noticed a new phenomenon relating to Honey's wellbeing. One day, Juliet drew my attention to the fact that parts of Honey's coat appeared to be changing colour. One side of her body appeared to be changing from her beautiful honey-coloured fur to a sort of dirty black appearance. Over the space of a few days the area of discolouration grew until it almost covered her whole right side, and we also noticed it had begun to appear on her other side too. I must admit we were rather worried but before rushing off to the vet, Juliet decided to enter her symptoms into a Google search, and she quickly found a possible solution. The Google search threw up an explanation together with photos which perfectly matched the change in Honey's fur.

It appeared that our little girl was suffering from something called *Seasonal Flank Alopecia.* a light-responsive condition that usually appears during the winter months and can last through to the spring. It usually lasts for up to six months and then it simply goes away as quickly as it first manifests itself. To be on the safe side, now that we felt we knew what the problem was, I made an appointment for Honey to see the vet, who in due course confirmed our home diagnosis. There is no known reason why this condition appears in any particular dog and in many cases a dog may suffer from it just the once, after which it can disappear, never to be seen again, or it can return on a regular basis year after year. The vet assured me however, that the condition didn't cause any physical symptoms apart from the obvious colour changes in the fur, so we were happy to know that Honey wasn't in any physical discomfort. In her case, it has returned every year, as regular as clockwork and we now accept it as a normal part of Honey's life. She does look rather strange for a few months of the year as her skin undergoes these regular changes, which always causes people and our friends to comment, obviously concerned for Honey's welfare. We are at least able to explain to them exactly what it is and that it will soon go away, which of course it does, almost like magic.

Honey and Muffin & Honey's Seasonal Flank Alopecia

HONEY OF COURSE had no idea that her appearance was changing during this seasonal problem, so it made absolutely no difference to her at all. She just carried on enjoying life, as indeed she should have done. None of the other dogs seemed to take any notice of her subtle colour change even as it continued to grow larger and larger as it spread. Before we knew it, the alopecia began to appear on her other side too. Poor Honey began to look like a patchwork quilt, but we loved her just as much as we always had done. By now of course, we knew that this was only a temporary condition, and it wasn't causing her any discomfort so we just ignored it, as it was the only thing we could possibly do.

Sure enough, as the warmer weather arrived, the alopecia gradually began to recede, and before we knew it Honey's coat once again appeared pristine, and she looked as gorgeous as ever. Many people and friends who'd seen the change in her appearance now began to remark at the apparently 'miraculous' conversion back to her original appearance. Honey just went on having fun, and before we knew it her third birthday came around and by then, we 'd forgotten about her skin problems.

Happy birthday Honey

Time had literally flown as far as Juliet and I were concerned. Honey was such a happy livewire of a dog. Her whole life just seemed to be one long playtime. I think I can honestly say that we'd never had such a permanently happy little dog in our home. Her tail just never stopped wagging. Either of us only had to say her name if she was lying down, sleeping, or just resting and she'd automatically spring into life and that tail would be wagging with happiness. Muffin, Digby, and Petal had definitely accepted her as part of their 'intimate circle' and they would happily allow her to join in their games, whether with them in a group or just occasionally playing with one or two of them. We often wondered why Digby meekly accepted one of Honey's favourite 'games'. She'd happily chase him around the garden until she'd eventually catch up with him and before he knew it, she'd have a hold of one of poor Digby's back legs, which she then proceeded to use like a 'chew toy', pulling and tugging on the leg, with Digby patiently allowing her the 'pleasure' of dragging him around the garden by the leg. Both Juliet and I wondered how and why he allowed her to get away with it, as we knew just how sharp Honey's teeth were and we couldn't understand how this didn't hurt Digby. Surely, we thought, one day she'll really hurt him, and he'll turn around and snap at her, but he never has, such is his enormous patience with the 'baby' of the family.

Gotcha! Honey playing tug with Digby's leg.

Honey really was, and still is, filled with boundless energy
and even when the other dogs decide they've had enough of
running, jumping on each other, and generally playing in the
garden or on the playing field, Honey just goes on, in her own

way, zooming around the field or in the garden just for the sheer joy of it. I can get tired from just watching her!

Zoom!!

The wonderful thing about Honey is that so far, she has never shown any signs of being ill and her only visits to the vet have been for her regular annual check-ups and booster vaccinations. It's a shame that the same can't be said for all of our dogs.

As a new year dawned upon us, Juliet noticed that Digby had developed a swelling around one of his teeth so, not wanting him to suffer from any pain, I phoned the vet and made an appointment for him to be seen. When we attended for his appointment, he was seen by Carolina, (she's Spanish and her name is pronounced Caroleena), who diagnosed a small abscess and recommended removal of the tooth at the same time as she removed the growth, and she made an appointment to see him in five days for the procedure to be carried out.

On the day of Digby's appointment, I dropped him off at the surgery bright and early at around 8.30 am and the poor little boy looked absolutely crestfallen as he became aware he wasn't coming home with me as I left him with the nurse after going through the booking-in procedure. I felt so guilty as I left the surgery without him, but I knew it was only for a few hours and he'd soon be home again. It was the standard procedure at our vets that they would telephone us when any operation was completed and the dog was in recovery, at which time I'd be given a time to go and collect our Digby.

When my phone rang at 2pm, showing the vet's number I presumed it would just be the usual call to tell me he was OK and give me a time to go and pick him up. However, when I answered the phone, it was Carolina, rather than the usual call from one of the nurses who was calling me. When she said there was a problem, I immediately expected the worst and that perhaps something terrible had happened to Digby while he was under the anaesthetic. In fact, she did tell me that there was a problem. The actual procedure had been successfully carried out but while he was under the anaesthetic, she'd taken the time to carry out a full examination of our little boy and had discovered a growth on his spleen. She told me that it was quite a large tumour and that she was going to refer Digby to the nearest specialist animal hospital, which was in Wakefield, about thirty miles away.

Filled with trepidation, I immediately asked her if she was saying that she thought Digby had cancer.

"I'm afraid so," she replied. "I've done scans and will be sending everything to the hospital who should be contacting you very soon to make an appointment for Digby to go and see them for an initial examination and they will then decide what course of action is required."

'Very soon' turned out to be the next day. The veterinary

hospital, *Paragon Referrals,* wasted no time in getting in touch with me. I received a phone call from them, and their senior oncologist spent a few minutes talking to me, after which he asked me to take Digby for an exploratory operation in three days' time. So began a worrying period for us, especially Juliet. Digby was her 'Mummy's boy' after all and the thought of losing him was almost too much for her to bear. The day arrived for me to take Digby to the hospital. Juliet had hardly slept the night before we went. She was truly terrified at the thought we might lose our gorgeous little boy. We set off early, allowing extra time for me to find the place when we got to Wakefield. It was a freezing cold February morning, and the journey would see me travelling on three different motorways and various dual carriageways. We were still in the middle of the Covid pandemic at that time so when we arrived, I had to park in the car park and phone reception and was told someone would come out to meet me. In a couple of minutes, the oncologist and a nurse both came out, and we walked Digby round the car park for a minute so he could get used to the strangers he was meeting for the first time. When the time came for me to leave him with them, he looked so sad as the nurse led him away from me, and I couldn't help becoming rather emotional and was really worried at what they might find. On the way home, as I passed a large lorry on the motorway, I saw a large piece of black plastic fall from the vehicle and I heard a loud bang as it passed under the car, and I saw it emerge behind me in my rear-view mirror. There didn't seem to be any obvious damage to the car, so I slowed down and continued with my journey, hoping to get home safely. When I eventually pulled off the motorway, parked in a lay-by, and examined the car, there appeared to be nothing visibly wrong with the car although I had noticed that there was a knocking sound when I applied the brakes. As soon as I arrived home, I told Juliet what had happened and immediately took the car to my local garage, who had been my 'go to' place for any work on my cars for over twenty years. I explained what had taken place to Andy, one of the two brothers who owned and ran the garage and also told him that I needed the car so I could travel back to Wakefield later in the day to collect a sick dog.

He immediately put the car up on the ramp and quickly identified the problem. Whatever had hit the car had dislodged a part of the braking mechanism. Not being technically minded I won't try to describe it here. It was almost lunchtime, when the garage would normally be closed from 1 till 2pm. Andy told me he'd do his best to have the car fixed in time for me to make the afternoon trip to collect Digby and I took a slow walk home and gave Juliet the news about the brakes. Imagine my surprise when I received a call from Andy at 2pm to inform me that he'd fixed the car and it was ready for collection. Bless him, he'd worked through his lunch hour to ensure that I'd have the car back in good time for me to go and collect Digby. When I arrived back at the garage and asked him how much I owed him for the repair, he replied, "No charge. All part of the service." Now, that's what I call fantastic customer service.

Not long after I arrived home with the car, Rodney, the oncologist called from Paragon. Juliet and I were so relieved when he told me that Digby didn't have cancer! (I'd put the call on speaker phone so Juliet could hear the news first-hand). However, he went on to explain that Digby did have a very large benign mass attached to his spleen that would have to be removed, along with the spleen which was irreparably damaged. Rodney gave me an appointment for five days' time and told me that I could expect to hear from Micky Tivers, their Head of Surgery, who would be performing Digby's operation himself. Digby was certainly receiving excellent care. He went on to inform me that I could collect Digby at 5pm that afternoon by which time he would be fully recovered from the exploratory surgery and the anaesthetic.

A couple of hours later, I once again made the trip to Wakefield and collected Digby, who I'm sure you can guess was overjoyed when he saw me waiting for him as the nurse brought him out to me. She handed me a packet containing a number of painkillers, just to help him through the next couple of days after the morning's procedure.

Juliet was of course overjoyed to see her little boy when we walked back into the house and all the other dogs made such a fuss of Digby. As dogs usually do, they sniffed him all over, as though they could smell 'vet' on him and there was a great deal of tail wagging from them and Digby as he was quite clearly pleased to be home, so pleased that when Juliet gave him his evening meal, he literally wolfed it down in record time.

The following day I received the expected call from Micky the surgeon who explained in detail exactly what Digby's operation would entail. He assured me that Digby would be fine after the operation and that dogs could survive quite happily without a spleen. After hearing what he'd told us, both Juliet and I felt much better and of course, over the next few days everyone, including the other dogs made such a lot of fuss of Digby. They seemed to be aware that something was wrong with Digby and little Honey, together with his sisters, Muffin and Petal, were being extra-attentive to him. They were still playing together but were also making lots of fuss of the little boy, cuddling up in bed with him even in the daytime, which at times tended to annoy poor Digby when he'd be snoozing in his 'day bed' in the utility room, only to suddenly find himself being almost buried under the 'caring' bodies of two or sometimes three dogs.

Honey cuddled up with Digby & Muffin

At least they were helping to keep him warm. Before we knew it the day of Digby's operation was upon us, and we woke up to find that heavy snow had fallen overnight, and I knew I'd need to set off early and drive very carefully in order to get to the hospital in time for his operation. Unfortunately, the snow continued to fall and by the time I should have been setting off, weather conditions were decidedly poor, so I decided to phone the hospital to see what conditions were like there. They explained that they'd also had heavy snowfalls overnight as well and that conditions in Wakefield were much worse than they were here at home and in fact, they had been about to call me to tell me that the surgeon, Mickey had been unable to get into work and that we'd need to reschedule Digby's operation, and we made a new appointment, and his operation was now fixed to take place in three days' time.

The day of Digby's revised operation dawned, and the

weather was vastly improved, so we had no problems in arriving in good time for our check-in at Paragon. I was met by the same nurse who'd checked Digby in on our previous visit and Digby seemed to remember her and allowed her to take him from me and he disappeared into the building with her, his tail wagging, which made me feel much better. At least he wasn't upset or apprehensive about me leaving him this time. Digby was scheduled to have the operation and would need to spend a night in the hospital so he could be monitored to ensure everything was alright after he'd been operated on.

I drove home and together with Juliet, spent the next few hours waiting for a call from Mickey, who'd promised to let us know how Digby was after the operation. Early in the afternoon my phone rang, and my caller ID showed it was *Paragon* calling. I was quite nervous as I answered the call. It was Mickey, the surgeon who instantly put my mind at rest by saying, "Hello Mr. Porter. You'll be pleased to hear that Digby's operation went perfectly, with no complications, and he's now in recovery."

I felt myself letting out a huge sigh of relief and then listened as Mickey went into more details about Digby's operation. He explained that although the 'mass' as he described it wasn't cancerous, it had been leaking poison into Digby's system and he was glad he'd operated when he did. It had become evident that if they hadn't operated when they did, and if the poison had continued leaking into his system, poor Digby would have probably been dead within a week. He also promised to send me some photographs taken during the operation, which he did, and I admit that Juliet and I were shocked to see just how large the growth had been, and we could see the poisonous stuff leaking into his poor little body. We were also amazed at the size of the operation scar. The incision was almost the entire length of the underside of Digby's body, but there wasn't a stitch to be seen!

Mickey had previously explained to me that there would be no visible stitches as any internal stitches they'd used would dissolve within his body, and externally they used a special glue to close the wound. How remarkable. I actually forgot to tell Juliet that bit and she would receive quite a shock when we got him home and she looked for the stitches. So, Mickey explained that I could collect Digby the following morning. He would be kept under observation overnight to make sure he was okay after the surgery. I asked if I'd have to take him back for any post-operative check-ups, and he said that wouldn't be necessary and that he would send all the details to my own vet, and they could carry out his post-op check and deal with any follow-up treatment. Juliet was relieved and delighted when I filled her in on my conversation with Mickey and we both slept better that night, though we were excited by the thought of bringing Digby home in the morning.

The following morning dawned, and we were struck by the 'curse' of Digby's operation again. We woke to a world encased in almost impenetrable freezing fog. You could hardly see your hand in front of your face.

"What will you do?" Juliet asked with a worried look on her face.

"Don't worry," I replied. "I'll set off in good time and take it really slow. It'll be okay, I promise."

"Please be careful, driving in this," she said as she pointed through the window at the murky grey scene outside.

Once I was ready, I kissed her goodbye and set off on yet another journey to Wakefield. As I wouldn't be outside for long, apart from when I was in *Paragon's* car park, and the Mercedes had a very good heater, I wore a polo shirt, with a sweatshirt and a fleece jacket. You'll soon see the significance of me describing my clothing for the journey.

Thankfully, everyone on the motorway was driving sensibly and at a much-reduced speed, I eventually arrived at my destination. Pulling up in the car in *Paragon's* car park, I pressed the button to open my driver's side window to allow some air into the car after my journey. I pressed the button to stop the window going all the way down and to my horror it carried on going down until it was fully open. Another press of the button and nothing happened. For some reason, my driver's side window was stuck in the fully open position and nothing I did could make it close.

A couple of minutes later, both Mickey and a nurse appeared with Digby who of course was overjoyed to see me, his tail wagging furiously with happiness. After giving him a minute to greet me, Mickey spent some time describing everything relating to the operation to me and giving me some advice for the future. He had a great sense of humour which he showed when he said to me, "At least you'll never have to worry about him getting cancer of the spleen in the future as he hasn't got one anymore."

The nurse passed me a small package containing some painkillers for Digby, enough to last him five days, by which time he should be pain free. After both Mickey and the nurse spent a minute giving Digby a cuddle and a final hug, we were good to go. Mickey's final words to me before we departed were, "Digby's an incredibly good dog. He's been the perfect patient, with such a warm and loving personality. It's been a pleasure to treat him."

With that, I thanked Mickey and the nurse, loaded Digby into the car and we set off for home, after I'd called Juliet to let her know that we were on our way, as well as telling her about the window. "Will you manage alright?" she asked me.

"I don't have much choice really. We'll be okay. I'll just have to take it slowly, so we don't freeze to death from the wind chill," I laughed.

The journey home was a nightmare to be truthful. I was only wearing the fleece jacket and the best I could do was put the collar up as far as I could to give me a minimum of protection from the freezing fog that still blanketed the country. I had the heater going full blast, but although it kind of kept my feet warm, it did nothing to stop my upper body and head becoming colder and colder as I drove home. There was poor Digby, in the back of the car, having just come out of the hospital after a major operation, with freezing fog being drawn into the car as I drove as slowly as I dared on the motorway. Luckily, there was a nice thick dog cushion in the back of the car, and he was wearing the lovely new coat we'd bought him to wear after the operation. I'd explained to the staff at Paragon that it wouldn't be practical for him to wear a buster collar as the other dogs would never leave him alone if he arrived home wearing one of those horrible things. The coat would help to stop him interfering with the operation wound and would now help to keep him warm on the chilly journey home.

We eventually arrived home, by which time the side of my face that had been constantly buffeted by the wind as we drove was completely numb from the cold. Juliet was of course delighted to see Digby and he was ecstatic to be home and he enjoyed the fuss and cuddles he received from Juliet. The rest of the dogs all gathered round, and it was obvious they knew something unusual had happened to him. They could of course smell 'vet' on him, and they all did their best to make a fuss of him, though we had to try not to let them get too fussy or start jumping on him in their excitement at seeing their friend home again. Juliet was extremely emotional to have her special little boy home safely but now my attention quickly turned to the car. We obviously couldn't leave it outside with the window wide open in an invitation to any car thief to steal the car, so after a quick cup of coffee to warm me up a little, off I went once again to our friendly neighbourhood garage. This time I saw Shaun, Andy's brother and he said he'd have a look at the window while I waited. After a few minutes, he finally managed to get the window to close by doing something to the switch and then slowly guiding it up until it finally closed fully. He explained that the problem lay in the switch, which would need to be replaced. He'd have to order the new one from Mercedes and in the meantime, he advised us not to use the switch. If we opened the window, it would once again open and remain stuck in the open position. The only thing I could do to prevent Juliet or me accidentally opening the window from habit, was to cover the switch with duct tape as a warning not to touch it.

A welcome home love from Mum

I was grateful to Shaun for doing the job while I waited and once again, when I asked him what I owed him, he said the same as his brother had on the previous occasion, "No charge, just part of the service." Perhaps you can see why we have used Descars for over twenty years. Thankfully, neither of us fell into the trap of trying to use the window until, three weeks later, the new switch arrived, and I was able to take the car back to the garage where the new switch was fitted, and all was fine once again. It was like a final closure to the saga of Digby's operation. In a footnote to the whole episode, I went back to the garage a few days later and when Shaun came out to see me, I pressed a sum of cash into his hand as a thank you from us for the excellent service he and his brother always gave us. He was reluctant to accept it, but I insisted, and he eventually took the cash, thanking me profusely and said it would keep him and Andy in coffee and biscuits for a month. I also paid a visit to our vet a few days later where Carolina carried out Digby's post-operative check-up, giving him the all-clear, much to my relief. I asked her to give me a hand getting him into the car, which was a small subterfuge to get her out of the surgery, to the car, where I'd kept a bottle of wine and a box of her favourite chocolates as a thank you from me and Juliet for saving Digby's life. If she hadn't carried out that examination while she had him under the anaesthetic for the tooth extraction, we'd never have known about that horrible growth in his body, and he'd have died within days. She was so grateful and said she was only doing her job, but I knew she'd gone the extra mile the day of the tooth extraction and I gave her a hug and pushed the gifts into her hands, leaving her standing there as I climbed into the car. I could see she was quite emotional as I drove off and saw her wipe a tear from her eye.

Now that he was safely home with a clean bill of health we could relax again and begin to enjoy normal life with the dogs once more. Honey of course was as delighted as the rest of the dogs to have one of her chief playmates home once again. Of course, as Digby was 'Mummy's boy', so Honey regarded herself as 'Mummy's girl' and she wanted to make sure she wasn't forgotten while Digby was of course receiving lots of attention after his operation.

As usual, Digby would jump up onto the sofa in the evenings for cuddles with Juliet, and Honey just had to force her way into those 'cuddle moments' whenever she could, as you can see from the following photograph.

Can I have a kiss too Mum?

She was actually intrigued by Digby's coat and spent a lot of time initially sniffing at it, trying to work out why he was wearing this strange thing in the house. She wasn't used to dog coats, as from being a little, tiny puppy she'd refused to wear a coat. Although we'd bought her some lovely warm ones she'd always made such a fuss about wearing one that in the end, we gave up trying to get her to walk along with a coat on as she just did everything she could to remove it, trying to rub it against walls or fences, rolling over and kicking her legs in the air, (which was so funny to watch) and Juliet became exasperated from trying to get her to wear a coat, so in the end she just gave up.

Digby continued to wear the coat for a couple of weeks while he recovered from his operation and Honey and the others soon got used to him wearing it constantly. The funny thing was that none of them ever tried to pull it or do anything that might damage it while they were playing together. We've often wondered if they somehow realised that the coat was in some way a part of whatever had happened to Digby, as we were certain they knew something was different about him at that time. In time, Digby's operation would lead to a change in Honey's daily routine, but for now all the dogs accepted that Digby had changed, albeit temporarily.

All friends together

Happy Honey

7

NEW ADVENTURES, NEW ROUTINES

DIGBY CONTINUED HIS RECOVERY, but this led to certain changes for Honey, as the vet had also insisted that Digby shouldn't do too much running or exerting himself for a few weeks after his operation. Up to this point, Juliet had always taken Honey along with Digby and/or Muffin and Petal together for their afternoon walk. It was Muffin more often than Petal, as Petal has always been the least energetic of the three siblings so when it came to running around and having playtime together or with other people's dogs, this arrangement made sense. She'd take Petal or one of the others on a separate walk, usually with little Cassie, who loved running and playing on the local playing field and even Petal could keep up with her and her short little legs.

Speedy Cassie

Even little Honey had longer legs than Cassie, though it was debatable whether she could run faster than our little Australian Terrier/Yorkie crossbreed.

Little Miss Sweet and Innocent

So, with Digby being slightly restricted for the time being, he'd be the one to regularly go with Cassie in the afternoons, while Juliet decided to alter the routine for the other dogs slightly. Petal and Muffin would now go together with Juliet, and the two of them could happily play together and with any of their doggie friends they might meet on their walk, and Juliet decided to devise a new afternoon walk for Honey.

It's worth mentioning that by this point in her life, Honey had become totally attached to Juliet and was also ultra-obedient to Juliet's commands. If Juliet told her to 'stay', she'd stay and if she called her back from any distance, Honey would immediately stop what she was doing and come scampering back at top speed to Juliet, only putting her 'brakes' on a few feet from her 'mum' and sliding to a stop right in front of her. Honey really is one of the best-trained dogs we've ever owned, a sheer pleasure to take for a walk, both on and off her lead.

Hi Mum, I'm back!

There are some very nice, picturesque woods quite near to where we live, and Juliet decided that, as she only had Honey to walk, it might be nice for Honey to have a chance to run free and play and explore the woods. This was probably the best thing Juliet has ever done for Honey. After a few days of this new afternoon experience for Honey, Juliet could hardly stop smiling and laughing when she'd return from these walks, which seemed to grow longer in duration the more she took our little girl to the woods.

She'd walk her on the lead until they arrived at the wood, and then she'd let her off to go ahead and explore this new place, full of strange sights and smells for Honey to investigate. After being a little hesitant to wander far from Juliet for the first couple of days, Honey soon began to feel at home in this new and exciting environment and Juliet would come home, full of stories about Honey's adventures.

The wood was home to all manner of small wildlife and Honey quickly got into the habit of sniffing and smelling around the bushes and trees looking for the source of some of these new scents she was picking up for the first time. Now that she'd discovered her confidence, Juliet would release her from her lead, and as she explained it to me, it was literally a case of 'Honey Unleashed' as our little dog would immediately set off at top speed, running and exploring, often disappearing from sight for a few seconds, though Juliet could hear her foraging in the undergrowth and bushes. One day, she came home and related a lovely story to me. Honey had disappeared for quite a while, and then suddenly appeared, running at top speed, chasing a poor squirrel. Juliet explained that she was a little worried as she definitely didn't want to see Honey catching and probably killing the squirrel, but of course, the squirrel was a clever, speedy and wily little beast, and it was almost as if it was having as much fun as Honey was, until all of a sudden, the squirrel came to a tree and before Honey knew what was happening, it scampered up the tree trunk until it reached one of the lower branches of the tree, leaving Honey bouncing up and down on her hind legs, doing her best to follow the squirrel up the tree trunk, unsuccessfully of course! Juliet called her, and sure enough, Honey immediately turned and came running back to her, finally stopping and sitting in front of Juliet, panting heavily and her tail wagging furiously. Honey had obviously thoroughly enjoyed herself and ever since that day, she's enjoyed many such encounters with the local wildlife, with squirrels, rabbits, an occasional hare and even a few stoats that have led her a merry chase through the undergrowth and the trees of our local wood, with the wildlife always being clever enough to elude the manic little terrier.

So, now you know where I got the idea for the title of this book. Seeing Honey dashing here, there, and everywhere in the woods is truly a sight to behold. As Juliet said one day, on returning from one of her afternoon forays with 'Miss Honeybun', "I've honestly never seen a little dog so happy and filled with joy, as Honey is when she's set free in the woods. She runs so fast her feet hardly seem to touch the ground." Sounds like a pretty happy little dog to me.

The other remarkable thing about Honey's visits to the woods is that she never, ever comes home dirty! Honestly, no matter how bad the weather, and it's often quite bad there in the winter, with many deep puddles, muddy patches, and soaking wet leaves etc, Honey seems to be impervious to dirt. Nothing sticks to her. Anyone could be forgiven for thinking she's received a coating of Teflon. I've seen her come home with Juliet, with Juliet's walking boots absolutely covered with wet, sticky mud and the bottoms of her black, waterproof trousers coated in mud which soon dries to a hard packed, filthy, muddy finish. At least the trousers are made for such treatment and a quick wash in the washing machine and they're as good as new. All Honey needs is a quick rub-down with a towel and she looks pristine. Even her pads, which you might expect to be rather muddy, look clean, absolutely nothing sticks to this dog! If she has got particularly wet on one of these excursions into her own little private 'jungle', all she does after a nice rub-down is find her favourite place next to the radiator in the utility room, where she'll spend a few minutes lying down and relaxing after all her happy exertions.

Of course, having had so much exercise tends to give her a healthy appetite and before long, she decides she's warmed up and has rested long enough and simply jumps up, shakes herself, wags her tail and trots into the kitchen, where she proceeds to try and play with the other dogs while Juliet and I prepare their food. I've often joked with Juliet. "Doesn't that dog ever rest for more than five minutes?"

Juliet's standard reply is, "Not until she's been fed, and we let her in the lounge."

In the evening our dogs are allowed in the lounge with me and Juliet and once they're in the room with us, they rapidly settle down and love nothing better than snuggling up on the sofa with Juliet or on the large armchair with me.

Drying off in front of the utility room radiator

Believe it or not, in spite of her diminutive size, Honey is actually quite heavy. Her weight now she's fully grown is fairly constant at around 20 kilograms. Some people have commented to Juliet that Honey is a bit 'fat' which is completely wrong. Honey is in fact very solid and when I took her to the vet for her annual booster vaccination, the vet herself, while giving her the usual annual health check, commented to me, "Wow, Mr Porter. This little dog is virtually solid muscle. She doesn't have an ounce of fat on her."

That pretty much put an end to any thoughts of Honey being fat or in any way overweight. When I arrived home and gave Juliet the news of the vet's description of Honey being 'solid muscle' she couldn't help laughing at the expense of those people who'd called her fat. She most definitely isn't. I'm pretty sure that a fat, overweight and obese dog could never run, jump, and play like Honey.

* * *

HONEY OF COURSE wouldn't have bothered in the slightest if she'd known what some people were saying about her, and she just carried on doing what most dogs do...enjoying life! Now, I think I should mention that just in case anyone is thinking that Homey could do no wrong...well, that wouldn't be completely accurate. Juliet would quite often come home after one of her afternoon long distance walks in the woods and tell me about Honey's occasional 'naughty' behaviour. This particular problem quite clearly manifested itself in Honey's 'possessiveness' towards Juliet.

Slimline Honey

IT WAS ALWAYS inevitable that at some point in her walks, she'd meet, and interact with other dogs. Usually, these meetings would be happy and peaceful, and Honey would be perfectly well-behaved...until...the dreaded moment would arrive when Juliet might meet someone with a beautiful little puppy for example. Still, there was no problem, and Honey would love it if the other dog's owner would come and make a fuss of her. After all, Honey must have thought, '*I'm so lovable, this is what I expect*' and everything would be fine. The problem would only show itself if Juliet then tried to make a fuss of the other puppy. Honey's tale would instantly stop wagging and she'd turn her lip up and start growling at the other poor, innocent dog. Juliet quickly realised what was happening and she'd stop stroking or making a fuss of the other dog. Immediately, Honey would stop growling, her tail would start wagging again and she'd literally pull on her lead, effectively dragging Juliet back to the other owner, (I told you she was strong), and she'd be quite happy as the other owner began stroking and fussing her once again.

"I'm so sorry," Juliet would apologise for Honey's jealous behaviour, but the other owner would invariably laugh at Honey's behaviour, usually responding by saying such things as, "She obviously doesn't want her Mummy making a fuss of any strange dogs, does she?"

"No, she doesn't," Juliet would reply but would usually add, "but it's rather embarrassing when I can't even give your dog a stroke without her being so naughty."

As time has passed, Juliet has tried everything she can think of to cure Honey of this possessive streak but sadly, she still exhibits the occasional jealous streak, except in the case of very young puppies who she rather likes and will occasionally try to play with. That's definitely an improvement.

Honey is just so playful and lovable and to be quite honest, she's never displayed any aggressive behaviour towards other dogs. I think she just likes to give them a little warning as if to say, "*She's MY mummy, so there!*"

That butter wouldn't melt look…hehe.

Pretty girl

8

SUNSHINE AND SNOW

HONEY'S fourth year was destined to be a rather eventful one, though we didn't realise it until the latter half of the year. From Honey's point of view, things couldn't have been better. She was such a happy little girl, and Juliet had also added a new nickname for her, as she was frequently referred to as *Honeybun*. She was, as always, such a happy dog, her tail always wagging happily, and I'm sure if she'd been human, her face would have had a permanent smile on it.

People often commented to Juliet that they'd never seen a dog that trotted along like Honey, when she was walking on her lead. Juliet did confirm to me that her tail would wag non-stop from the moment she left the house, all the way through her walk, and she had such a lovely 'spring' in her step as she walked.

As for playing with the rest of our dogs, every day was just a non-stop game for Honey. I'm sure Muffin, Digby and Petal must have felt totally worn out by the end of the day, as Honey never seemed to leave them in peace for more than a few minutes, and even when she did, she'd simply turn her attention elsewhere, usually towards Sheba. Despite her age, and the fact that she was suffering quite badly with osteoarthritis, fifteen-year-old Sheba was always so happy, and ready and willing to play, which always amazed me and Juliet.

Honey and Sheba

Happy Sheba

By this time, Sheba was no longer able to go for proper walks any more as her legs just weren't strong enough, so I bought a beautiful new dog stroller for her, and she loved going out with me and Dylan every day for rides around the village. Lots of people would stop us and make such a fuss of her and Sheba just loved all the attention she received on her walks around the village.

Her disabilities certainly didn't stop her enjoying life and she loved playing in the house and garden with Honey and the other dogs of course. The previous year Sheba had developed a very large abscess on her face just below her right eye, and the vet had diagnosed it as a benign tumour, and we agreed to an operation to remove it as it was growing larger and would have begun to interfere with her vision. After the operation, the vet sent the tumour to the laboratory for testing, just to be on the safe side, and we were shocked when the results came back to say that the growth was cancerous.

The vet was as surprised as we were and gave us a number of options, one of which would have involved the removal of Sheba's eye. We considered everything and bearing in mind Sheba's age and state of health, we decided to not have any operations or other interventions on the cancer. We'd loved her and cared for her from the time we'd found her in the dog pound, close to death and she was so happy that we decided to let her live her life out normally and face whatever the future may bring.

A year later we were astounded to find that there wasn't a trace of cancer. Somehow, our beautiful Sheba had beaten it. So, despite the osteoarthritis, she was fine in all other respects, as evidenced by the way she'd roll around on the floor, allowing little Honey to jump all over her, often joined by the other dogs in a great big 'doggy pile-on'. It was so funny to watch them playing together, as Sheba had always looked quite ungainly when she'd roll over onto her back, even though she always had that incredible staffy smile on her face, which always told us she was happy and having a great time.

As summer drew to a close everything seemed to be going well for our little pack. Honey continued having great fun, playing with our other dogs and with those she'd meet while out and about on her walks with Juliet.

Group sunbathing

Honey could have just as much fun in the house and garden as she could out on her walks. Happiness just seems to be her middle name. I can truthfully say that I've never seen Honey looking down or depressed apart from short periods when she's reacted to the loss of any of our dogs, her playmates. She'd certainly felt the loss of Sasha and took quite a while to get over the fact that Sasha had suddenly disappeared from her life, but her wonderful ability to integrate with the other dogs, and the way she'd made herself a part of the 'musketeers' had quickly helped her to get over that loss. Dogs really are so resilient.

Fun in the garden with Juliet

Summer soon gave way to autumn and before we knew it, another birthday came around, and our little Honey was now four years old.

Happy 4th birthday Honey

Four years had virtually flown by. Juliet and I could scarcely believe that the little Christmas present that Victoria had surprised us with had grown up and was now without a doubt a fully adult dog, though to watch her in action you could be forgiven for believing that Honey was still little more than an adolescent puppy. Honey appeared to have decided that her mission in life was to bring and to spread happiness wherever she went. Various people continued to comment to Juliet, saying that they'd never seen a dog walking down the street the way Honey did, with her tail profusely wagging at top speed with every step she took. It usually took people meeting her for the first time, no more than a few seconds to fall in love with this little bundle of joy. Honey of course just loved the attention she'd receive from people she met for the first time. Her little face would literally light up with joy and her tail would go into overdrive as soon as anyone started to make a fuss of her. Juliet would always come home after a walk with Honey, with a big smile on her face. Honey was such a great source of happiness and joy.

* * *

BEFORE WE KNEW IT, the colours of autumn, that beautiful transition from the brilliant hues of summer as the leaves on the trees went from green, through browns and gold, and the flowers in the garden began to fade and die for another year, and gradually gave way to winter. Summertime officially ended as the clocks were put back an hour and daylight hours grew shorter. Temperatures dropped and it was time for Juliet and me to take our winter coats, boots, and scarves out of the wardrobes.

I'd often joked when talking to the dogs, saying "It's okay for you guys, you've got built-in fur coats. Me and your mum aren't so lucky." It's worth mentioning that the area where we live is relatively sheltered from the worst of the British weather. We live in an area known as the Vale of York, which was at one time a glacial valley where now, the towns of Wetherby, Tadcaster, Northallerton and of course the city of York are located. So, when much of the country is subjected to heavy snowfalls, we tend to get off lightly, with, in general only slight falls of snow, except in the few areas of higher ground.

You'll recall my description of the weather we faced at the time of Digby's operation. The snow at that time was some of the heaviest we'd seen for years, just our bad luck that I'd had to travel to Wakefield at that time. What I forgot to mention while describing my journey's back and forth with Digby for his treatment at the animal hospital in Wakefield, was that this coincided with Honey's first experience of snow.

Most dog owners will, I'm sure, agree with me when I say that the majority of dogs just love snow! They love rolling in it, playing in it, and generally have a fantastic time frolicking in the white stuff. So, how did little Honey react to her first snowy experience?

That first morning when we awoke to find our back garden blanketed in pure white, virgin snow, and I opened the door to let the dogs out at around 6am, they all seemed to sense the change in the weather, and it was as if they knew that snow had magically appeared overnight. They went bounding out of the door into the garden and the virgin snow was virgin no longer! They loved it and it was instant playtime, all except for one of the dogs...Honey.

What's this white stuff?

Poor little Honey followed the rest of the dogs out through the door as usual, surely expecting to go zooming down the garden for a quick play session before breakfast. But all of a sudden, she came to an abrupt halt. Obviously, this white stuff that covered the garden must have felt strange beneath her little paws, cold and slippery. I smiled and called Juliet from the kitchen and together we watched to see what she'd do next. As the other dogs were all happily playing in the snow, she decided to try walking slowly on the snow to see what the others were doing. By the time she reached the bottom of the garden the others were really enjoying themselves in the snow. Muffin, Petal, and Digby in particular were having a great time. Honey still wasn't sure and as you can see from the above photo, she just stood there, looking unsure of what to do next. I felt sorry for her. Usually, our dogs instinctively seemed to know that snow provided a great source of fun, but Honey was proving to be an exception to the norm. That is, until Muffin and Petal decided it was time she joined in the fun.

Fun in the snow with Muffin and Petal

Muffin and Petal were having a play fight in the snow, and then, as they saw little Honey standing looking miserable all by herself, they must have decided to involve her in their game. Muffin suddenly turned and leapt on Honey, one of their usual ways of beginning a playfight, and Petal quickly joined in. Honey instinctively reacted and before she knew it, she was romping with the two sisters in the snow. It had taken a few minutes for her to get used to the feel of the snow beneath her paws and now that Muffin and Petal had enticed her to join in their fun, she at last realised that snow was nothing to be afraid of and before we knew it, she was running around and playing with the rest of the dogs.

Once she'd got used to it, it was soon evident to us that she loved it and from that time, whenever we have a snowfall, Honey's now the first out of the door, 'leading the charge' to go out and play. It's a shame we don't get more snow in our area because even when it does snow here, it's usually nothing more than a light dusting of the stuff, not really enough for serious dog play, but those few days around Digby's operation it was definitely deep enough for the dogs to have a great time on their walks on the playing fields, or in Honey's case, on her walks in the woods. Juliet came home from one such walk one day and told me how Honey had such a great time in the woods. She was doing her best to run around and kept disappearing behind the trees, then suddenly reappearing with her snout covered with snow, a sure sign that she'd been burrowing into the snow beneath the trees and under the bushes. Her tail was wagging furiously, and the look on her face was one of pure joy. I've often regretted that Juliet isn't very good at using the camera on her phone, as she has, unfortunately, missed numerous opportunities to capture some great photos of Honey on her 'walks on the wild side'. Juliet said that she'd given Honey a stroke and told her she was a good girl for coming back to her Mum, and

Honey promptly zoomed away again, at top speed, her short little legs propelling her in little hops and jumps through the thick snow, which was obviously much deeper in the woods than it was in our back garden. Yet again, Honey proved to be impervious to the effects of snow, much like she is to rain, as despite all her romping around in the woods or on the field, she still remained perfectly clean. Nothing seemed to stick to her coat. She's probably the nearest thing we've ever found to a 'waterproof' dog, or at the very least, she's seriously water resistant. A quick rub down with a towel once she gets home and she's ready to go out and do it all over again! I always find it amusing when they come home and often Juliet will ask me to give her a rub down.

I just call out, "Honey, tummy rub' and she knows exactly what I'm saying, as she runs up to me, sits at my feet, and when I take a dog towel down from one of the hooks in the utility room she virtually throws herself down on the floor and rolls over onto her back, paws in the air, ready for me to give her a really good belly rub. When I've finished, she stands up and I give her a final rub by running the towel under her body and quickly rub backwards and forwards, and she absolutely loves it. That tail of hers just never stops wagging. What a wonderful, happy little dog she is.

Once the ritual of the tummy rub is completed, Honey invariably runs outside and spends a few minutes enjoying herself in the garden, either playing with one or more of the other dogs or just amusing herself by doing insane zoomies all over the garden. Eventually she appears to tire herself out and decides to come back indoors, where I'm usually sitting at the dining table enjoying a cup of coffee. Not wanting to be ignored, she often arrives close to where I'm sitting and if she feels she's not getting the attention she deserves, I will suddenly feel two little paws resting on my leg as she jumps up and demands some of that attention, and I spend a minute or two stroking and loving her as she continues wagging her tail, enjoying the fuss she's receiving.

That loving feeling

Honey on the run

9

A TOUCH OF SADNESS

AS THE YEAR drew towards its close, and our lives continued much as they always did, we began, as most families do at this time, preparing for the upcoming Christmas holidays. With Rebecca and Victoria both now grown up and living away from home, Christmas Day would be a quiet one, with just Juliet, me, and the dogs together to enjoy the festivities. Rebecca was at University in Leeds, studying Accountancy and Victoria was living in Newcastle, with a really nice young man, where she had a very good job working in management for a well-known home alarm company, so we were happy that they were both doing well in their chosen careers.

As it can be difficult teaching dogs to understand the meaning of Christmas, since the girls left home, Juliet and I make sure that the dogs enjoy their normal routine on Christmas Day, with some nice treats thrown in of course. So, they get their normal morning walks and again their usual afternoon exercise too, meaning there isn't really time for us to prepare and enjoy a traditional Christmas dinner at lunch time. Instead, whatever we decide to have for our main meal on the big day is reserved for the evening, when all the dogs have had their walks and their usual meal. Once they've all settled down, it's then 'our time' when Juliet and I can prepare and enjoy our Christmas Dinner.

I am, however, jumping the gun a little, as it wasn't quite Christmas yet. It was late October when we noticed a sudden deterioration in Penny's health. Poor Penny had suffered from arthritis for a number of years and had slowed down considerably in recent months. She spent most of her time in the lounge with Cassie, as we considered the other dogs to be a bit too boisterous for Penny as she grew older and frailer. Penny and Cassie were the best of friends, and we'd often see them playing together in the lounge during the day, Cassie always doing her best to encourage Penny, though poor Penny would often tell Cassie off if she didn't feel like joining in with Cassie's little games. The two of them would usually cuddle up together at bedtime and when Juliet and I woke up in the morning, the first thing I would see as I went to go down the stairs, would be Penny, standing at the bottom of the stairs, with her tail wagging, waiting for me to go downstairs to let her out into the front garden, and of course, she'd be closely followed by Cassie.

One morning however, as I looked down the stairs, I saw Penny as usual, but I instantly knew something was wrong. I called Juliet who came out of the bedroom, and she instantly saw what I'd seen. Poor little Penny was doing her best to stand up, but her back legs weren't working. She tried and tried, and it was heart-breaking to see and both Juliet and I knew instantly that her back end had collapsed. Her legs had given up on her and when I reached her and tried to help her to stand, my poor Penny just collapsed as soon as I let go of her and removed my support from her. I gently picked her up and took her out to the garden where she managed to go to the toilet, after which I brought her indoors and placed her in her bed, where she relaxed a little.

We both realised the end had come and with great sadness, a couple of hours later, I had the sad duty of taking our beautiful, always happy little Penny to the vet where she was gently put to sleep for the final time, as I held her in my arms, cuddling her close to my body as she slipped away. There were lots of tears cried that morning from Juliet and me as we mourned the passing of our little girl who we'd adopted so many years ago and who was sixteen years old when we said goodbye to her for the last time.

Happy Penny in younger days with her ball.

Anyone who has read Penny's story in the fourth book in this series, *Penny the Railway Pup* will know how Penny loved running and playing with a ball, and how she had great fun at the seaside, where she'd have great fun playing and swimming in the sea and romping on the beach with Dylan. She was always such a happy little dog and it's difficult for me to write about her, even now, without feeling great sadness as I remember all the happy times we had with little Penny.

Memories of Penny

As if losing Penny wasn't bad enough, just a few weeks later, our gorgeous Bedlington Terrier, Dylan, who was also 16 years old, also passed away, exactly a week before Christmas. Dylan, who had gradually gone deaf and blind in his later years, never let those disabilities affect him and right up to his final week, he enjoyed going for two walks a day, during which he'd accompany me and Sheba, who would be in her stroller. Dylan was so confident walking beside me and trotting along with Sheba in her stroller. People we met on the streets could scarcely believe that he was blind and deaf when they met him for the first time. His tail would be wagging, and he knew just where we were on our regular walking route, even knowing exactly when to stop when we reached our regular 'treat stops' without me needing to utter a word of command.

Young Dylan, (all paws clear of the ground, our 'Flying Bedlington')

Sadly, in that fateful last week, he suddenly went off his food, and became disinterested in going for his walks. It was obvious to both me and Juliet that all was not well with our little boy, and each day it was evident to us that he was rapidly growing worse. By the end of the week, poor Dylan had reached a point where he'd stopped eating and could hardly make it out into the garden to go to the toilet and we knew his time had come. I had to make yet another heart-breaking journey to the vet with my poor Dylan wrapped in a blanket and I literally held him in my arms, cuddled close to me, so he knew I was with him, (remember he was blind and deaf), and stroked and loved him as the vet sent him on his final journey to the Rainbow Bridge. He'd been with us for all those years, and it caused both Juliet and me much sadness and we cried so many tears at losing Dylan so soon after Penny.

As a result, Christmas was quite a muted affair for us and even our other dogs seemed to sense that Juliet and I were very sad and upset at the time. Even Honey, our non-stop bundle of joy knew something had happened and of course, they all realised that there were some 'missing faces' in our home. Honey especially, suddenly decided that the time was right for her to give her 'mum', Juliet, some extra-special loving attention and when she jumped up on the sofa for her evening cuddles with Juliet, she would literally snuggle up as close as she possibly could and would 'treat' Juliet to extra sloppy kisses and would virtually wrap her paws around Juliet's neck with all her weight on Juliet's chest. Talk about empathy. We were convinced that Honey was doing all she could to console and love Juliet through her grief over the loss of both Dylan and Penny.

It took a few weeks for us to recover from the double loss of both Penny and Dylan and the house now felt quite empty to Juliet and me. We had gone from having eleven dogs just a couple of years ago to now having only seven, which might seem a lot to some people but to us, it was a vast reduction in the number of paws we had padding around the house. Every dog has its own individual personality of course and with each loss, there always seemed to be something missing in the house, apart from the physical presence of the dogs that had crossed the Rainbow Bridge. It's very difficult to try and explain how we felt but I suspect that most dog lovers will understand what I'm getting at.

Cuddles with Mum

Life of course returned to normal, or perhaps it would be better if I describe it as a 'new normal'. Certainly, it made a big difference to our daily dog walking routine. As I used to be the one who walked Penny and Dylan, it left me with fewer dogs to take out on our twice daily walks. Sheba definitely missed

Dylan who used to accompany her on her trips around the village in her stroller. Despite being blind and deaf, Dylan had always walked bedside Sheba's stroller, fully confident as long as he could sense me holding on to his lead. Most people we met and talked to would express their surprise when I explained that Dylan could neither see nor hear them, so confident did he appear to any casual observer.

Sheba and Dylan

Our lives seemed to be changing at a dramatic pace. Juliet and I, having spent so many years loving and caring for all our dogs, were now being faced with the inevitable losses that were unavoidable as age and infirmity began to catch up with the senior members of our doggy family. No matter how much effort we put into keeping our dogs happy and healthy, we couldn't keep the years at bay, and it wasn't long before we were faced with yet another tragedy. Less than three months after losing Dylan, poor Sheba's osteoarthritis finally took its final toll on her. Sheba had always been so happy and cheerful, even with her disabilities but one morning when we went downstairs, we could tell she was struggling. Our poor little girl simply couldn't get up and even though her tail was wagging in happiness at seeing us, it was obvious to us that we couldn't let her go on struggling. She'd spent many happy hours playing with her best friend, Sasha and with little Honey from the time she'd joined the family.

Honey and Sheba

It was truly heartbreaking for me to have to take our beautiful Sheba to the vet that day. All the staff at the veterinary surgery had known her for many years and had been involved in her treatment virtually from the day I first took her in after we'd adopted her. Having had a terrible start in life, being used as a bait dog by an evil dog fighting ring, we'd managed to save her and give her a long, happy life, which finally came to an end at the age of fifteen years. I've honestly never seen Juliet cry so much as she carried Sheba to the car and gently laid her on the blanket in the back, and loved and cuddled her as she said her last goodbye. In many ways, probably because of the terrible start she'd had in life and the amount of love and care we'd lavished on her in the beginning in order to make sure she survived, we both treated Sheba as one of the most special dogs we'd ever brought into our home and losing her had a devastating effect on both of us.

With Sheba gone, our family of rescue dogs was now reduced to just six dogs. Now, some people might think that six dogs is still a lot to deal with, but believe me when I say that for Juliet and I, our house really did feel empty at times. In a comparatively short period of time, we'd lost Dexter, Sasha, Penny, Dylan and Sheba, and our canine family now consisted of little Cassie, now the eldest at the age of seventeen, Muttley, now nearly thirteen, Digby, Petal and Muffin, all ten, and the 'baby' of the family, who has recently celebrated her fifth birthday.

We were actually quite surprised at Honey's reaction to Sheba's loss. Despite her age and infirmities, Sheba had always been such a happy dog and had continued to do her best to interact and play with the other dogs right to the end of her life. Honey in particular had always loved playing with Sheba, who had enjoyed rolling around on the floor with Honey, the two of them so often engaged in a rather clumsy version of roly-poly as Sheba was always quite ungainly when she was on her back, but she loved having little Honey clambering all over her and her tail would be wagging furiously as Honey would nudge her with her nose in an attempt to get Sheba to play with her. It was quite hilarious to see them together.

All of a sudden, Sheba was no longer there and Honey certainly seemed to realise quite quickly that one of her playmates had disappeared from the house. We both noticed how, over the first couple of weeks without Sheba, Honey was walking around the house and garden as if she was searching for her friend. Most touchingly, Sheba would often spend time in the evenings lying next to the front of the sofa, where she'd happily lie there, snoozing and relaxing. One evening, I noticed that little Honey was lying in exactly the same place as Sheba used to do and I mentioned this to Juliet. We both thought this was quite touching and at first we thought this could have just been something of a coincidence, but when Honey continued the identical behaviour over the next few weeks, we both felt that this was Honey's way of retaining some kind of connection with her friend. Eventually, she seemed to have accepted that Sheba was no longer with us and she returned to her usual place on the sofa, cuddled up as close as she could get to Juliet. This often led to some amusement, as both Honey and 'Mummy's Boy' Digby would both try to get as close to Juliet as they possibly could, which often led to Juliet being virtually squashed under the weight of two dogs lying across her legs or even her chest. Sometimes, just to vary the routine, Digby might be a little slow in claiming his place on the sofa and little Muffin would somehow force herself into place with her Mummy, but of course, Honey would make sure that she had pride of place and it would amuse me to see poor Muffin being virtually crushed beneath Honey as she positioned herself on top of Muffin and I could only imagine how Juliet must have felt with the combined weight of the two dogs happily snuggled up across her.

Squashed Muffin

Of course, with Sheba gone, Honey still had plenty of play-mates, both at home and during her daily walks with Juliet. Honey was of course extremely protective towards Juliet, one could actually say she was extremely jealous if any strange dogs approached Juliet and although Honey has never been aggressive towards any other dogs, she could definitely find ways to 'warn off' any dogs that attempted to get too close to Juliet. She'll sometimes bark to tell the interloper off and it could be quite hilarious to see her literally turn her back on another dog, blatantly ignoring it if it came too close to 'her' Mummy. The exceptions to this type of behaviour came in the form of some of Juliet's dog walking dog friends, most of whose dogs Honey had known since she was a little puppy herself and who she'd kind of grown up with. In addition, we discovered that Honey actually loved puppies and if a friend, or a new acquaintance appeared while Juliet was out walking with Juliet, with a new puppy in tow, Honey would quickly do her best to make friends with the puppy. Puppies of course loved to play with Honey and Juliet would come home quite frequently with tales of Honey's latest new 'doggie friend'.

As I've previously mentioned when talking about Honey's playtimes with Muffin, Digby, and Petal, she can be quite boisterous in her playtimes with the other dogs in the family and Juliet was often quite worried that Honey would accidentally hurt any new puppy that she decided to play with. She needn't have worried, thankfully, as Honey seemed to instinctively know the difference between a puppy and a fully grown dog, and I was impressed when Juliet would come home and relate to me how gentle Honey was in her interactions with any new puppies she'd made friends with. For some reason, puppies didn't appear to make Honey jealous, and she'd happily 'allow' any new puppies to play with Juliet without appearing in any way put out by Juliet making a fuss of the puppy. It really does make you think just how a dog's mind works sometimes.

Beautiful Honey

10

ANOTHER FRIEND DEPARTS

WITH ALL THE changes that had taken place during Honey's life with us, she might have been forgiven if she occasionally became confused by the sudden disappearances of some of the dogs who'd been her constant companions since she'd joined our family. Of course, dogs do tend to be very resilient, and most are able to adjust quite well when any of their closest 'friends' are no longer around. In Honey's case she has always been very quick to adjust as our family of rescues has shrunk in size.

One thing Juliet and I soon noticed after losing Sheba, was that as well as her usual time spent playing raucously with Muffin, Digby and Petal, Honey seemed to be spending more time with Muttley than she had previously. If you've read the previous book in the series, *Muttley's Tale*, you'll know that poor old Muttley, who we adopted as a puppy, came with certain problems that nobody could have envisaged at the time we brought him into our home and family. Most important among these problems was the eventual discovery that Muttley, unusually for a dog, suffered from agoraphobia, something neither Juliet nor I had ever heard of as affecting dogs. Our vet explained that though rare in canines, it was something that could affect them quite badly and needed careful care and management. How we handled Muttley's affliction is explained in his book, and we're pleased to say that after a lot of careful management, and lots of love and affection, together with great patience, Muttley was able to live a pretty normal and happy life.

His problems tended to make him something of a loner, even within our family of rescues and it was so sad for him that his closest doggie friends, Dexter, Sasha, and Sheba, all passed away one after the other, and he could have been forgiven if he'd become withdrawn and lonely. He used to cuddle up with Dexter at night as he did with Sheba after Dexter's passing, but with Sheba gone we wondered how he'd cope without her closeness.

You can perhaps imagine our surprise when, one morning, Juliet and I came downstairs just after 5.30 am to discover Honey and Muttley cuddled up in bed together. Had Honey sensed Muttley's loneliness and decided to show him some affection? Could it be a mere coincidence that she'd found her way into the bed with him? Perhaps it had been cold in the night and the two of them were merely seeking warmth from one another? We'd have to wait and see. Over the next few days, we'd come downstairs in the mornings and sure enough, on most of those mornings, Honey and Muttley were happily snuggled up in bed together. They even spent time together during the day, often just getting together for a snooze. We couldn't help noticing that after appearing to be quite lonely and depressed for a time after Sheba's passing, Muttley's tail had got its wag back!

It was wonderful to see Honey becoming great friends with Muttley. They made something of an odd pairing, the totally extrovert Honey and the quiet and reserved Muttley. We knew how close the pair had become when we found them lounging in the sunshine, side by side in the garden.

Honey snuggled up with Muttley.

By now, Honey had celebrated her fifth birthday. We could hardly believe how time had flown. It only felt like a few months had passed since that gorgeous little puppy had entered our home for the first time.

Juliet and I simply loved this little bundle of energy who just loved life, with her constantly wagging tail and her irrepressible desire to enjoy life, every single day. Honey loved attention of course, as most dogs do, but it was her ability to make friends with any dog or any human that was and still is her most endearing quality.

As we come nearer to the current date, and Honey's story comes towards its close, it's sad to have to tell of yet another loss in our canine family. On the 28th of February, we celebrated Muttley's 13th birthday, and everything seemed good in our world. Unfortunately, a week after his birthday we noticed that all wasn't well with Muttley, and we could tell our little boy wasn't well. A visit to the vet followed and we were devastated when Yolanda, the vet informed us, after performing a number of tests, that he was suffering from liver failure. This was the same disease that had taken our Dexter from us over three years ago and here we were, being faced with the same thing once again. The vet prescribed the necessary drugs and a new prescription diet which Muttley appeared to respond to, and we dared to hope that, like when Dexter was first diagnosed, he would have a good amount of life ahead of him. Sadly, it wasn't to be, and on the day before Good Friday, Muttley suffered from a sudden deterioration, and I had to rush him to the vet. Tests showed that our poor boy was bleeding internally, and we had no choice other than allowing the vet to put him to sleep, and Muttley passed away peacefully in my arms as I loved and cuddled him with tears running down my face. It all happened so suddenly and despite the fact that we knew he was unwell we certainly never expected him to be taken from us so suddenly. This happened just a few days ago so you can imagine how I'm feeling having to include such sad news in Honey's story.

When I arrived home from the vets without Muttley that evening, the first thing Honey did was to look for her friend. She went out into the garden, and we could tell she was searching for him. She just couldn't settle down for the rest of the evening and we felt awful for her at bedtime when she would normally wait for Muttley to get into bed and would then climb in with him, snuggle up and the two would go off to sleep together.

Goodbye to our dear Muttley.

Over the last few days and nights, she has gradually adjusted to missing her friend, and now seems to have realised that Muttley won't be coming home. Juliet has assured me that she's totally normal when she goes out for her daily runs and she's once again enjoying playing with Muffin. Digby and Petal.

If anything, she's tormenting the three of them more than ever!

A beautiful sketch of Honey

11

HONEY MEETS HEIDI

WITH THE LOSS of poor Muttley, our family of rescue dogs was now reduced to just five dogs. We still had little Cassie, who is now 17 and will hopefully celebrate her 18th birthday later this year, and of course there was Muffin, Digby, and Petal, who are now ten years old, and Honey remained the 'baby' of the family at five years old.

We could only hope that our remaining doggy family continues to be fit and healthy for a long time to come. In the meantime, Juliet had brought up the subject of perhaps bringing another dog into our family. Though it was still quite soon after the loss of Muttley we'd probably wait a little while before going into the subject seriously, or so I thought.

We both knew that the one thing we'd have to consider if we did decide to look for a new addition to the family would be Honey's attitude towards other dogs. She's so attached to Juliet and as we've seen, she can often display jealousy if Juliet makes a fuss of other dogs they meet on their long walks. So, the only way to avoid bringing a dog into the home that Honey might reject, will be to make any new addition a puppy, as of course, Honey seems to rather like little baby dogs. Perhaps they bring out her own 'mothering instinct', presuming of course that she has such a thing.

She really is such a wonderfully happy, playful little dog and she obviously has many years of happy times ahead of her. So, if and when we did bring another new dog into our family, we'd have to hope that he or she has the requisite energy to keep up with Honey and the others. The new puppy would need lots of energy to enable them to fit into the family and I know that Honey and the others would be the perfect playmate for a playful puppy. Whatever breed it might be, it would never be short of playmates, being surrounded by Honey, Muffin, Digby, and Petal, and despite her age, I'm sure little Cassie would be raring to go once she realised there's a new puppy on the premises.

A new sketch of Cassie

So, the search was on for the next dog to join our happy family. All we had to do is find a puppy that would be 'acceptable' to Honey. There are so many breeds to choose from and in this case, it won't be quite the same as adopting a new rescue dog.

A brand-new sketch of Honey on the run

Over the years, as my regular readers will know, obtaining a new addition to our doggy family has usually involved a visit to one of our local dog rescue or animal sanctuaries. Searching for a puppy would be a very different experience for Juliet and for me. We had no specific breed in mind when we began our search, and Juliet enlisted the help of our friend, Malcolm, who was himself searching for a new addition to his small dog family which currently numbers just two rather large shaggy, black dogs, though I'm not sure what breeds they are. Juliet must have mentioned to him that when we first got together, I owned two dachshunds, because, before we knew it, he was regularly sending her links to various websites, almost all of which were exclusively dedicated to the sale of dachshund puppies. Even though I kept repeating to Juliet that I thought it might be a bit too soon to think about bringing another dog into the family, she wouldn't be put off, and before long I was being regaled with picture after picture of various dachshund puppies for sale in our area.

I DID my best to reject or politely ignore advert after advert until one day, around a month ago, Juliet brought my attention to one particular post on Facebook, advertising dachshund puppies for sale in our area. Most of the previous adverts had featured beautiful puppies, but all had been what I considered to be ridiculously expensive. This one, however, quoted a more reasonable price and I had to admit they were all gorgeous little puppies, and my interest was aroused. I happened to notice that at the top of the advert was a little box that said, 'See next advert' and as a matter of interest and as a comparison I clicked on the box and found another litter of dachshund puppies which were a slightly lower price and this time, something about the photos of this particular litter definitely piqued my interest. When I read the information provided, I saw that there was only one unsold puppy left in the litter and I instantly showed it to Juliet who agreed that the unsold puppy was a beautiful little dog with unusual silver-coloured markings. The advert contained a phone number, and I agreed that Juliet should phone the seller and request further information about the unsold puppy.

Photos from the original advertisement

The lady who answered the phone explained that the puppy had been the 'runt' of the litter and was much smaller than her siblings. Juliet kept looking across at me as she talked to the lady as if imploring me to take this seriously. When she asked if we could go and see the puppy, the lady explained that we could view the puppy by video call as she didn't usually allow people to visit her at her home due to the fear of dog thieves. Juliet explained who we were and that we were totally trustworthy and asked if the lady would make an exception just this once. She must have sounded sincere, because the lady agreed and Juliet put me on the phone and the lady, who said her name was Julie, gave me her address and directions to her location, which happily, was only a ten-minute drive away from our home. I invited my friend Malcolm to accompany me to view the puppies as he'd been the one helping Juliet by doing all the searching for a suitable puppy.

When we called at Julie's home to see the puppy, I was immediately smitten by the little, tiny pup that Julie was holding in her arms. Julie invited us in and when we walked into the lounge we were met by the sight of the rest of the litter, happily playing together on the floor. Julie explained that they were all sold, except for the one we'd come to see, and were awaiting collection on the coming Wednesday when they'd be 8 weeks old and ready to leave their mother.

She explained that the puppy, (who we'd already decided to call Heidi), had been the runt of the litter and had almost died at birth. The mother dog had experienced difficulty in giving birth to this, the last of the puppies and Julie had assisted her with the birth. Heidi had been so tiny and wasn't breathing at first, so she'd helped get the puppy breathing. Little Heidi had been so small that Julie basically hand-reared her for the first two weeks of her life, eventually placing her with the rest of the litter, where she fitted in with her siblings immediately. She then introduced me to the parent dogs, Albert and Hazel, who both made such a fuss of me, and I could tell they were happy, well-adjusted dogs and I knew that Heidi was the dog for us.

I paid the deposit and made arrangements to pick up the little dog on Wednesday. Subsequently, little Heidi became the latest member of our canine family, and we hoped our other dogs would have no problems in accepting the new addition. We needn't have worried, as we carefully introduced the new baby to our other dogs over a 24-hour period and within two days we were amazed to see that all our dogs had instantly accepted Heidi into the pack and were happily playing with their new puppy friend.

Digby was the first to show his acceptance of the puppy, on the very first day, he virtually adopted the tiny pup, being so gentle with her and allowing her to cuddle up to him in his bed, and even began tentatively playing with her. The rest of the dogs soon followed Digby's example and much to our surprise, Honey also accepted little Heidi very quickly, and before long it became apparent that of all our dogs, she had become Heidi's new best friend. This was exactly what we'd hoped for, as poor Honey had lost so many of her doggy friends within the family, with Sasha, Sheba and Muttley all departing for the Rainbow Bridge. With the rest of our dogs all being considerably older than Honey, our fear had been that one day, she could be left as our only dog, and that would have been a terrible situation. Now, with Heidi's arrival, Honey will have a great playmate for years to come, not that we expect any of the others will be leaving us any time soon.

Watching Honey and Heidi playing and interacting with each other, even at this early stage of Heidi's life with us, gives us great confidence that it won't long before Honey and Heidi will soon be running and having fun together on the playing field and enjoying long walks in the woods together, so maybe it won't be long before 'Honey Unleashed' becomes 'Honey and Heidi Unleashed'.

Heidi

In the years to come, as Heidi grows up and becomes a fully-fledged member of our doggy family, I'm sure the time will come when I'll be sitting down to write her story, but for now, that's something for the long-distant future. I feel it's perfectly fitting therefore, that I close Honey's story with some lovely photos of her, and our other dogs, enjoying playing with the latest addition to 'the pack'.

Digby and Heidi

Petal and Heidi

Muffin and Heidi

Of course, we must close this little gallery with Honey herself, enjoying playing with her new best friend. Hopefully, as Heidi grows up, she and Honey will grow closer and closer to become the very best of friends and will enjoy many happy years together.

* * *

HERE'S a lovely photo of Honey and Heidi snuggled up together at the end of another long, gruelling day of happy play-times and enjoyment. We may have lost most of the dogs who were part of Honey's early years with us, but of course, she's still surrounded by the 'three musketeers', of Muffin, Digby, and Petal who we hope will be around for quite a lot of years to come and who she'll continue to have great fun with. Cassie is nearly 18 years old now and prefers pretty much to be left to her own devices, though she still loves running around on the playing field near our home, so Heidi really signifies a whole new generation for our pack and maybe in the next couple of years, there could be another new face or two arriving in our home. Only time will tell.

What better way to bring Honey's story to a close than with her safely and happily cuddling up with our beautiful new puppy, as the arrival of Heidi signals the beginning of yet another new chapter in the lives of our family of canine companions? I hope you've enjoyed reading *Honey Unleashed* and hope to see you again soon.

Time for bed

GALLERY

I hope you'll enjoy viewing the following gallery of photos showing Honey in various situations, including some from the various dog websites on Facebook that have featured our beautiful girl.

3 Years Old!

Honey

Mascot of Day

Honey

Happy Birthday

PIC·COLLAGE

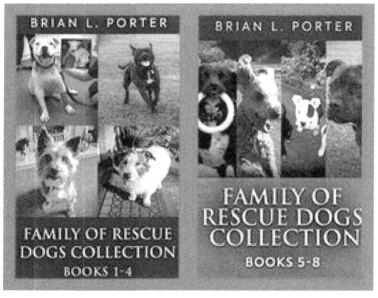

AUTHOR'S NOTE

A Tale of Two Dachsunds?

As I mentioned at the beginning of Honey Unleashed, this was originally intended to be the last book in my Family of Rescue Dogs series, but, in conversation with many of my readers, it's clear to me that people still have a desire to read about our dogs. It's logical to assume that at some time in the future, our latest puppy, little Heidi will have a story to tell but that could be a few years away. Meanwhile, I might be able to write another book about the dogs that were already with me when Juliet and I first met. Fittingly perhaps, with the arrival of Heidi, my two constant companions when Juliet came into my life were a beautiful pair of dachshunds, a gorgeous long-haired girl by the name of Sophie, and a mischievous little smooth-haired dachsie named Candy. Together, we shared some wonderful happy times, and maybe, just maybe, there's another story to tell. So for now please, watch this space...

Candy and Sophie

ACKNOWLEDGMENTS

I owe my thanks to quite a few people who had a part in helping me to create *Honey Unleashed*. As always, I owe a massive debt of gratitude to my lovely wife, Juliet, not only for her input into the book itself, but for her daily efforts in keeping our family of rescue dogs fit, fed, exercised, and well-groomed. There's no way I could look after all the dogs by myself, and she carries the burden of walking most of them, now that my health prevents me walking them as I used to, restricting me to walking the older, slower, and infirm members of the pack, so none of these books could be written without her.

To all the staff at Vets4Pets in Doncaster, I owe thanks for their continued care, when required, for all our dogs. Their courteous, caring, efficient and professional service has helped to care for our dogs for over twelve years, and my dogs have always been treated like VIPs, (Very Important Pets), from the moment they step through the doors.

Finally, it goes without saying that Honey's story could not have been written without the daily input from the rest of the dogs who make up our wonderful pack of rescues. Their interactions with Honey have helped to make her story 'come to life.'

ABOUT THE AUTHOR

 Brian L Porter is an award-winning author, and dog rescuer whose books have also regularly topped the Amazon Bestselling charts, twenty-six of which have to date been Amazon number 1 bestsellers. Most recently, one of his latest Dog Rescue Books, *Muffin, Digby, and Petal, Together Forever,* was voted the Best Indie Book of 2021 by the readers of Readfree.ly website. And his Cold War thriller, *Pestilence,* was announced as the winner of the Readfree.ly Best Book We've Read all Year Award for 2021, an award also won by *Remembering Dexter* in 2019. The third book in his Mersey Mystery series, *A Mersey Maiden* was voted The Best Book We've Read All Year, 2018, by the same organisation. *The Mersey Ferry Murders* has also recently won the Best Mystery Novel Award in the Critters Annual Readers Poll 2021.

Last Train to Lime Street was voted Top Crime novel in the Top 50 Best Indie Books, 2018. *A Mersey Mariner* was voted the Top Crime Novel in the Top 50 Best Indie Books, 2017 awards, and *The Mersey Monastery Murders* was also the Top Crime Novel in the Top 50 Best Indie Books, 2019 Awards Meanwhile *Sasha, Sheba: From Hell to Happiness, Cassie's Tale and Remembering Dexter* and *Muttley's Tale* have all won Best Nonfiction awards. Writing as Brian, he has won a Best Author

Award, a Poet of the Year Award, and his thrillers have picked up Best Thriller and Best Mystery Awards.

His short story collection *After Armageddon* is an international bestseller and his moving collection of remembrance poetry, *Lest We Forget*, is also an Amazon best seller.

His children's books, *Alistair the Alligator*, *Charlie the Caterpillar*, and *Wolf*, written under the Harry Porter name are all Amazon bestsellers.

Last but not least, his collection of romantic poetry, *Of Aztecs and Conquistadors*, written as Juan Pablo Jalisco is also an international Amazon number 1 Bestseller, topping the bestselling rankings in the USA, UK, and Canada.

Rescue Dogs are Bestsellers!

In a recent departure from his usual thriller writing, Brian has previously written eight bestselling books about the family of rescued dogs who share his home, with this book being the 9th in the series.

Sasha, A Very Special Dog Tale of a Very Special Epi-Dog is now an international #1 bestseller and winner of the Preditors & Editors Best Nonfiction Book, 2016, and was placed 7th in The Best Indie Books of 2016, and *Sheba: From Hell to Happiness* is also now an international #1 bestseller, and award winner as detailed above. Released in 2018, *Cassie's Tale* instantly became the best-selling new release in its category on Amazon in the USA, and subsequently a #1 bestseller in the UK. Most recently the fourth book in the series, *Penny the Railway Pup*, has topped the bestseller charts in the UK and USA. The fifth book in the series, *Remembering Dexter* won the Readfree.ly Best Book of the Year 2019 and has gone on to win another two awards, the first of Brian's books to win more than two literary awards. The sixth book in the series *Dylan the*

Flying Bedlington has already won a first nonfiction book award.

Muttley's Tale actually achieved a bestseller ranking in Australia soon after its publication.

If you love dogs, you'll love these nine illustrated offerings with *Honey Unleashed* now added to the list.

Many of his books are now available in audio book editions and various translations are available.

Brian lives with his wife, Juliet, and their wonderful pack of (sadly reduced) six rescued dogs in the north of England.

To learn more about Brian L. Porter and discover more Next Chapter authors, visit our website at www.nextchapter.pub.

FRON INTERNATIONAL BESTSELLING
AUTHOR BRIAL L. PORTER

The Mersey Mysteries

A Mersey Killing

All Saints, Murder on the Mersey

A Mersey Maiden

A Mersey Mariner

A Very Mersey Murder

Last Train to Lime Street

The Mersey Monastery Murders

A Liverpool Lullaby

The Mersey Ferry Murders

Under a Mersey Moon (Coming soon)

Thrillers by Brian L Porter

A Study in Red – The Secret Journal of Jack the Ripper

Legacy of the Ripper

Requiem for the Ripper

Pestilence, Breathe if you Dare

Purple Death

Behind Closed Doors

Avenue of the Dead

The Nemesis Cell

Kiss of Life

Dog Rescue (Family of Rescue Dogs)

Sasha

Sheba: From Hell to Happiness

Cassie's Tale

Penny the Railway Pup

Remembering Dexter

Dylan the Flying Bedlington

Muffin, Digby, and Petal, Together Forever

Muttley's Tale

Honey Unleashed

Newly Released

Family of Rescue Dogs Books 1-4 Box Set

Family of Rescue Dogs Books 5-8 Box Set

Short Story Collection

After Armageddon

Remembrance Poetry

Lest We Forget

Children's books as Harry Porter

Wolf

Alistair the Alligator, (Illustrated by Sharon Lewis)

Charlie the Caterpillar (Illustrated by Bonnie Pelton)

As Juan Pablo Jalisco

Of Aztecs and Conquistadors

Many of Brian's books have also been released in translated versions, in Spanish, Italian and Portuguese editions.

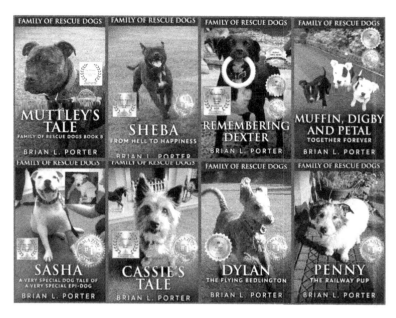

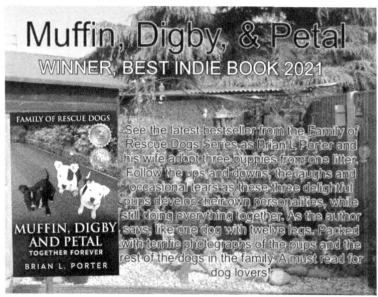

Printed in Great Britain
by Amazon

27863123R00098